MW01012501

EXTRAORDINARY RECIPES FROM

SEATTLE CHEF'S TABLE

JAMES O. FRAIOLI

THE EMERALD CITY

Food Photography
by Jessica Nicosia-Nadler

LP

LYONS PRESS
Guilford, Connecticut
An imprint of Globe Pequot Press

Lyons Press is an imprint of Globe Pequot Press.

Photography by Jessica Nicosia-Nadler unless otherwise credited on page 191.

Text design: Libby Kingsbury
Layout artist: Nancy Freeborn
Project editor: Julie Marsh

Library of Congress Cataloging-in-Publication Data is available on file.

ISBN 978-0-7627-7359-6

Printed in the United States of America

10 9 8 7 6 5 4 3 2 1

Restaurants and chefs often come and go, and menus are ever-changing.
We recommend you call ahead to obtain current information before
visiting any of the establishments in this book.

To the wonderful city of Seattle and the Eastside.
Thank you for being one of the greatest places to live in the world.

Contents

Fish & Shellfish

Acknowledgments

James O. Fraioli would like to personally thank the following people for their generous support and assistance with this book:

Sagiri Arima for her countless hours of research, support, and dedication.

Food photographer extraordinaire Jessica Nicosia-Nadler.

Chef John Hall and the amazing culinary team at Le Cordon Bleu College of Culinary Arts–Sacramento, California: Chef Jessica Williams, Chef Jason Murchison, Chef Robert Siegmund, Chef Sandra Washington, Patricia Nicosia, Torrey Crable, Amber Raffile, Thomas Pfingston, Christopher Thompson, Brien Kuznicki, Andrew Shoneff, Jimmy Johnson, Eli Darnell, David Pompey, Caroline Elias, Jessica Atkinson, Micah Tasaki, and Patrick Schwent.

Mary Norris and Katie Benoit at Globe Pequot Press, Literary Agent Andrea Hurst, and last, but certainly not least, all the contributing chefs and restaurants. Without their support and assistance, this book would not have been possible.

Introduction

There's a famous saying here in town, "People in Seattle don't tan, they rust." This saying is true, unfortunately. Seattle (originally called New York by settlers in 1851) is well known for its drizzles and downpours. The skies are often dreary, the winds are often howling, and just when a ray of unexpected sunshine peaks through a stratocumulus cloud, a threatening storm rushes in, sealing off the light. But for those of us Seattleites who are impervious to rain ("liquid sunshine" as we like to call it), a beautiful city exists beneath the clouds. It's no surprise that readers of *Travel+Leisure* and *Condé Nast Traveler*, two of the world's foremost travel magazines, voted Seattle one of their top ten favorite cities to visit. Seattle is a dynamic, creative city that's deluged with famous rock stars, Fortune 500 companies, awe-inspiring scenery, and some of the best coffee shops, restaurants, and eateries in America.

In Seattle you haven't had enough coffee until you can thread a sewing machine while it's running.

JEFF BEZOS, founder of Amazon.com

Known as the "Emerald City," in reference to the lush evergreen forests of the region, Seattle continues to birth culinary innovation and success. We have Seattle's Best Coffee, Starbucks, and Tully's, along with endless espresso roasters and cafes, all in pursuit of making and serving what they believe is the "best" cup of coffee. We have the world-famous Pike Place Market, one of the oldest public farmers' markets in the country. This top destination and Seattle tourist attraction first opened in 1907 and continues to serve as an epicenter for fresh local ingredients. And we have outstanding restaurants, hundreds of them scattered throughout Seattle like raindrops, and plenty more on the Eastside (that's the name for the inland cities reached by crossing one of two floating bridges over Lake Washington, if you're not from around here). Some of the best restaurants—forty-six of them to be exact—are highlighted in this cookbook.

Seattle is home to renowned chefs, including Food Network chefs and James Beard Award–winning chefs, all with an eye on the stove, the weather, and the calendar. All are eager to take advantage of the distinct seasons the Northwest brings to this sublime city tucked in the far corner of the United States away from the rest of the country (that's what the East Coast thinks, anyway).

Springtime in the Pacific Northwest is recognized for tender asparagus, delicious sweet peas, ruby red stalks of rhubarb, along with fresh cold-water shrimp and white-bellied halibut pulled from the icy depths of the neighboring Pacific Ocean. Summer (yes, there really is a summer here, and it's magnificent!) is filled with fresh-caught chinook, coho, and sockeye salmon, meaty Dungeness crab, aromatic herbs, and lusciously plump blackberries and blueberries bursting with flavor. Fall in Washington is harvest season for prized edible wild mushrooms like morels and chanterelles; bright, crisp apples; and many leafy greens. Winter showcases an abundance of fresh mussels and oysters, particularly the delicious Penn Cove varieties; beautiful lentils; alder-smoked fish; and finely aged cheeses.

From the early Scandinavians who came to fish and log in the Seattle area, and the Japanese who operated truck gardens and hotels, to communities of Italians, Chinese, Jews, and Filipinos peddling their wares, Seattle is extremely diversified, especially when it comes to cuisine. There's an International District located downtown, home to several Asian ethnic groups, where just about anything Asian inspired can be purchased,

prepared, and cooked. Nearly every country of the globe is well represented on Seattle's menus. The city's culinary reputation owes just as much success to the thriving ethnic communities as it does to the abundance of local produce, organic meats, and, of course, fresh seafood.

Without question Seattle is proud of its culinary presence, which seems to have started when the inundation of Microsoft money in the '90s created a demand for a more expansive and creative restaurant scene. And so we pay homage to the picturesque city of Seattle, the Eastside, and the extraordinarily talented chefs and restaurants residing within. Restaurants were chosen for inclusion in this book based on their perfect balance of ambience, customer service, and inspired cuisine.

No matter how sophisticated dining patrons are these days, one thing remains true (other than the predictable weather): Seattle remains a small informal city where warm and friendly service exists. Unlike New York or Los Angeles, where waiting lists for upscale restaurants can be hysterically annoying, diners in Seattle can actually get a seat at the places they read and hear about. On behalf of all the notable chefs and restaurants, I hope you receive great pleasure from the recipes in this book and will share them with your family and friends; may you also someday find yourself strolling down a weathered pier on the Seattle waterfront or along Old Main Street in Bellevue, reminiscing about the delicious meal you just experienced or envisioning one you are about to enjoy. Until then, delight in these tantalizing photographs and tastes from Seattle's best restaurants. *Bon appétit.*

NORTHWEST BITES

Seattle's diverse cultural makeup and proximity to the Pacific Ocean and its world-class seafood make for some of the best dining in the Northwest, beginning with delectable bites and nibbles to begin one's extraordinary dining experience. Because Seattleites love to eat at fine steakhouses, fish restaurants, Italian eateries, and pretty much anywhere that spends time crafting incredible food, the pages ahead offer a sampling of Seattle's most popular restaurants along with their most requested bites—all of which are delicious and easy to make at home.

Seattle's Andaluca Restaurant and Bar starts it off by offering zesty spicy calamari and its best-selling crispy duck cakes, while Cactus enjoys a Mexican flair with its crisp and colorful ceviche and bacon-wrapped jalapeños. For locals, happy hour at Daniel's Broiler means three things: great atmosphere, great cocktails, and great food. Two of its most sought-after happy hour bites are the filet mignon steak strips and the spicy barbecued prawns.

Of course, any mention of Seattle restaurants must include crab, so notable Chandler's Crabhouse makes a splash here with its award-winning Dungeness crab cakes and savory Dungeness Crab & Artichoke Dip. For newcomers to Seattle, or longtime residents seeking a change of scenery, stop by Joey's for a bite. Its eye-catching Chicken Jalapeño Corn Dogs are sure to please. The same is true of Purple Café and Wine Bar. Just don't forget to order its famous Baked Brie with Candied Walnuts & Caramelized Onions.

Andaluca Restaurant and Bar

407 Olive Way, Seattle
(206) 382-6999
www.andaluca.com
Owners: Birney and Marie Dempcy

Step out of the cold, drizzly Pacific Northwest weather and take a seat inside the comfortable and cozy Andaluca Restaurant and Bar. Rich mahogany seating and colorful hand-painted murals help create a destination-like setting. The Mediterranean decor is a preview of the fun Mediterranean-inspired dishes that are a warm, welcoming sight to locals and vacationers alike.

Situated inside the historic 1926 Mayflower Park Hotel, one of the oldest hotels operating in the heart of downtown Seattle, Andaluca Restaurant and Bar is led by Executive Chef Wayne Johnson. The former Kentucky native, who was recently featured on the Food Network's *Iron Chef America*, invites you to sit back, relax, and try his many signature dishes, ranging from refreshing garden gazpacho, flavorful crab cakes, and crisp tender quail, to perfectly seared Alaskan halibut and seafood paella. "Paella is one of my favorite foods to make," adds Chef Johnson, who likes to embark on trips through the Mediterranean to hone his culinary skills and perfect such dishes. "Paella is a great dish to feed a crowd and keep them happy." At Andaluca Restaurant and Bar, you'll find the food is always fresh, innovative, and served with a smile.

SPICY CALAMARI
SERVES 4–6

4 tablespoons olive oil, divided

1 cup diced onion

2 teaspoons fresh minced garlic

1 teaspoon red chili flakes

1 teaspoon kosher salt

2 cups pureed tomatoes

2 teaspoons lemon zest

2 teaspoons chopped fresh rosemary

1 teaspoon tomato paste

1 pound fresh calamari, sliced into rings and tentacles

2 tablespoons minced fresh Italian parsley

Pour 2 tablespoons olive oil into a large sauté pan. Over medium-high heat, add the onions, garlic, red chili flakes, and salt. Sauté until the onions are soft and translucent, about 3 minutes. Add the pureed tomatoes, lemon zest, rosemary, and tomato paste and cook for 5 additional minutes.

In a separate sauté pan, add the remaining 2 tablespoons olive oil. Over high heat, add the calamari and sauté until the calamari is opaque, approximately 2 minutes. (Be careful not to overcook, as the calamari will become tough.) Remove the calamari from the sauté pan and transfer to the hot tomato sauce. Stir to combine and let stand for 20 minutes at room temperature. Stir in the parsley.

Serve chilled.

CRISPY DUCK CAKES WITH APRICOT CHUTNEY

MAKES 16 CAKES

Duck Cakes:

1 cup fine bulgur wheat

¾ cup boiling water

½ teaspoon 3:1 ratio (kosher salt to sea salt) salt mix

1½ teaspoons olive oil

1 pound ground duck meat

1 onion, cut into ¼-inch dice

1 tablespoon minced garlic

¼ cup minced fresh Italian parsley

¼ teaspoon ground allspice

1½ teaspoons 3:1 ratio (kosher salt to sea salt) salt mix

½ teaspoon fine ground black pepper

½ teaspoon chopped toasted pine nuts

½ teaspoon minced fresh lemon zest

1½ teaspoons ground cumin

1 teaspoon ground coriander

1½ teaspoons minced marjoram

1 ounce olive oil for frying the cakes

1 teaspoon fresh chopped chives for garnish

Cucumber Raita:

32 ounces (4 cups) plain yogurt

1 cup peeled, seeded, and diced cucumber

2 tablespoons fresh chopped fresh cilantro

2 tablespoons fresh chopped fresh dill

2 tablespoons fresh chopped fresh mint

2 tablespoons fresh chopped fresh green onion

2 tablespoons chopped roasted garlic

1 teaspoon 3:1 ratio (kosher salt to sea salt)
   salt mix

1 teaspoon fresh orange zest

1 cup peeled and finely diced carrots

1 cup finely diced red bell pepper

Apricot Chutney:

⅓ cup diced onion

1 teaspoon minced garlic

½ teaspoon black mustard seed

½ teaspoon 3:1 ratio (kosher salt to sea salt) salt mix

1 teaspoon minced fresh ginger

1 cinnamon stick

1 pinch ground cloves

⅛ teaspoon red chili flakes

⅓ cup cider vinegar

¼ cup brown sugar

1 tablespoon honey

2 tablespoons sugar

1 bay leaf

1 pinch dry thyme

6 cups chopped fresh apricots, skin left on
   (dried apricots can be used)

2 fresh oregano sprigs, for garnish

To make the duck cakes: In a mixing bowl, combine the bulgur wheat, boiling water, salt, and olive oil. Let sit for 1 hour at room temperature, until the water is absorbed.

In a separate mixing bowl, combine the ground duck meat, onion, and garlic.

In another mixing bowl, combine the parsley, allspice, salt, black pepper, pine nuts, lemon zest, cumin, coriander, and marjoram. Toss well to combine. Transfer this mixture to the bowl with the ground duck meat and mix well to combine. It is essential that the spices are evenly distributed without overmixing the meat.

Using an ice-cream scoop, scoop the meat into 1-ounce balls. Hold enough of the soaked bulgur wheat in your hand to coat the cakes. Press the duck cakes into the bulgur, coating the entire cake while forming a patty shape. Patties should be about 2 inches in diameter and about 1 inch thick. Transfer the patties to a deep pan layered with wax paper so the patties don't stick together. Do not layer more than 2 layers deep or the duck cakes will get smashed. Place the patties in the refrigerator.

To make the cucumber raita: Combine all the ingredients for the raita in a large mixing bowl. Whisk by hand until well combined. Place raita in the refrigerator.

To make the apricot chutney: In a large saucepan over medium-high heat, add the onion, garlic, mustard seed, salt, ginger, cinnamon stick, cloves, red chili flakes, cider vinegar, brown sugar, honey, sugar, bay leaf, and thyme. Boil for 10 minutes. Add the apricots, reduce heat to simmer, and cook for an additional 15 minutes (when working with fresh apricots, discard any liquid before incorporating fruit into the pan; if using dry apricots, add 3 to 4 cups of the saucepan liquid to a bowl and add the dried apricots to rehydrate them; then simmer for 20 to 25 minutes instead of 15). Transfer to a shallow pan and let cool.

Add the olive oil to a flat-top griddle or large frying pan over medium-high heat. When hot, carefully add the duck cakes. The cakes should not move while cooking, or the bulgur will fall off. Cook the cakes for 3 minutes on each side, or until crisp and golden brown. Remove from heat.

To serve: Place 3 duck cakes on the center of each serving plate and sprinkle with chopped chives. Spoon some apricot chutney alongside. Top the chutney with oregano sprigs. Transfer the cucumber raita to a small sauceboat and serve immediately.

CACTUS

4220 EAST MADISON STREET, SEATTLE
(206) 324-4140
WWW.CACTUSRESTAURANTS.COM
OWNERS: MARK AND BRET CHATALAS

Around the corner from the Seattle Arboretum and Japanese Garden is Madison Street. Follow this quaint neighborhood street to the end, where pavement meets the lapping shores of Lake Washington, and you'll arrive in Madison Park, which is home to a number of shops, boutiques, and restaurants, including Cactus.

The restaurant first opened its doors twenty-two years ago, offering the young, active suburbanites of Madison Park a creative new spin on traditional Mexican, Southwestern, and Spanish cuisine. Cactus was the first Seattle-area restaurant to feature tapas, which were new to the food scene at this time. Instantly the south-of-the-border-style food caught on, and Cactus lovers across the lake inquired as to when a second restaurant would make its way to the "east side" of the city. In 2002, owners Mark and Bret Chatalas opened a second Cactus location across the 520 bridge in Kirkland, another popular neighborhood for the young and active, that boasted stunning postcard views of Lake Washington. Four years later, a third Cactus location opened at Seattle's famed Alki Beach. And, most recently, a fourth location welcomed residents, tourists, and business folk at South Lake Union.

Regardless of which waterfront location you choose for dining, one thing is certain: The food is consistent and lives up to its billing. Zesty guacamole, grilled jalapeños, and blue corn calamari definitely add zing, while the hand-stuffed chiles rellenos, sizzling

fajitas, and house chimichangas—filled with your choice of natural chicken, carnitas, or homemade chorizo—are sure to please. Of course one cannot forget the tropical libations, which are staples at Cactus. Whether it's a refreshing margarita or summer mojito, the signature cocktails at Cactus are crafted using fresh juices, herbs from the garden, and top-shelf liquors—the perfect choice when kicking back with friends.

Ceviche

SERVES 4–6

10 ounces fresh sea scallops, thinly sliced

6 ounces fresh skinless/boneless Pacific snapper, thinly
   sliced into 1- to 2-inch pieces

1 cup fresh lime juice

1½ teaspoons chopped lime zest

½ cup rice wine vinegar

2 tablespoons sugar

1½ teaspoons minced serrano chiles

1½ teaspoons kosher salt

1 teaspoon coriander seeds, toasted and ground

1 cup loosely packed ⅛-inch-thick red onion slices

½ cup loosely packed chopped fresh cilantro
   (save some sprigs for garnish)

1 cup cored, seeded, and diced Roma tomatoes
   (about 3 or 4 tomatoes)

Tortilla chips

Guacamole (fresh)

In a large glass or plastic container, add the scallops, snapper, lime juice, lime zest, vinegar, sugar, chiles, salt, and coriander. Gently mix to ensure all ingredients are evenly distributed. Refrigerate for 4 hours, then gently strain the seafood and discard the liquid.

Place the seafood, red onions, cilantro, and tomatoes in a bowl and gently fold them all together until evenly mixed.

To serve, mound the seafood in the center of the bowl and garnish with a cilantro sprig. Serve with tortilla chips and fresh guacamole.

GRILLED BACON-WRAPPED JALAPEÑOS

MAKES 20

Pickled Jalapeños:

20 fresh jalapeños

3 cups distilled white vinegar

3 cups apple cider vinegar

2 cups cold water

1 medium carrot, sliced into 1-inch pieces

1 yellow onion, peeled and cut into quarters

4 whole garlic cloves

1 sprig fresh thyme

4 bay leaves

1½ teaspoons whole black peppercorns

1½ teaspoons coriander seeds

1½ teaspoons kosher salt

1 (20-ounce) package bacon, cut into
   approximately 4-inch pieces

Relleno:

4 ounces softened goat cheese

5 ounces softened cream cheese

½ teaspoon finely chopped rosemary

½ teaspoon finely chopped thyme

½ teaspoon finely chopped sage

½ teaspoon finely chopped Italian parsley

Buttermilk Crema:

¼ cup buttermilk

1 clove garlic

½ cup sour cream

To make the pickled jalapeños: In a large pot over high heat, combine the jalapeños, white vinegar, cider vinegar, water, carrots, onions, garlic, thyme, bay leaves, peppercorns, coriander, and salt. Cover the vegetables with a couple of plates or clean kitchen towels so they stay submerged. When the pot is about to boil, remove from the stove. Remove the plates or towels and pour all

the ingredients into a glass or plastic container. Place the plates or towels back on top of the vegetables so they stay submerged. Place the container in the refrigerator overnight. The next day, remove the plates and cover the container until ready to use.

To make the relleno: Combine the goat cheese, cream cheese, rosemary, thyme, sage, and parsley in a bowl, and mix to evenly incorporate the herbs.

To make the buttermilk crema: In a blender combine the buttermilk and garlic. Blend until the garlic is finely minced and incorporated into the buttermilk. Transfer the buttermilk and garlic mixture into a bowl and fold in the sour cream until all of the ingredients are incorporated.

Drain the pickled jalapeños and pat dry. Using a paring knife, cut a small slit in the side of each jalapeño and remove as many of the seeds as possible while maintaining the shape of the pepper. Using a pastry bag or small spoon, stuff the jalapeños with the relleno. The jalapeños should have their original shape and should just barely close. Wrap a piece of bacon around the middle of the jalapeño so that it just barely overlaps. Place a toothpick through the bacon and jalapeño at the point where the bacon overlaps.

Place the jalapeños on a hot grill over medium heat, turning them several times while cooking so that the bacon cooks evenly. Grill for 4 to 5 minutes, or until the bacon is evenly cooked through and the inside is melted and hot.

Transfer the jalapeños to a platter and drizzle with buttermilk crema.

Daniel's Broiler–Lake Union

809 Fairview Place North, Seattle
(206) 621-8262
www.schwartzbros.com
Owner: Schwartz Brothers Restaurants

Simply referred to as "Daniel's" by locals, Daniel's Broiler has been a Seattleite staple for years. It is the restaurant of choice among those who want fabulous food amid an attractive and lively setting. At the Lake Union location, arriving by pleasure boat, mooring dockside, and strolling up to the outdoor restaurant deck is how one does it in style. But you don't need an expensive watercraft to visit Daniel's. You just need a willingness to have fun and an appetite for some of the best prime steaks and succulent seafood in the state.

Happy hour at Daniel's, whether at the Lake Union location or at Bellevue Place or Leschi Marina, is always en vogue. Well-dressed men and women crowd the piano bar, especially on Friday and Saturday nights, sipping stylish drinks (or enjoying one of the many wines on its *Wine Spectator*–award-winning list) and appreciating some of the best appetizers in town, including the Prime Filet Mignon Steak Strips and the Spicy Barbecued Prawns. The steak strips—cooked under an 1,800°F flame—is a Daniel's favorite.

"For best results, marinate the filet mignon for at least twenty-four hours," says Executive Chef Mike Hillyer. The Spicy Barbecued Prawns is another Daniel's signature. "The spice blend gives this dish its fiery kick and can also be used as a rub for seafood and chicken on the grill." Daniel's is also known for its fresh seafood such as Australian rock lobster tails and wild Alaskan king salmon.

PRIME FILET MIGNON STEAK STRIPS

SERVES 2–4

¾ cup soy sauce

¼ cup water

⅛ cup pineapple juice

½ cup brown sugar

1 teaspoon grated fresh ginger

1 garlic clove, peeled and finely chopped

2 tablespoons olive oil

1 pound filet mignon, cut into 1-inch cubes

¼ cup chopped green onions, optional

Toasted sesame seeds for garnish, optional

In a mixing bowl combine the soy sauce, water, pineapple juice, brown sugar, ginger, garlic, and 1 tablespoon oil. Place the filet mignon cubes in a gallon-size freezer bag. Pour the marinade in the bag, coating the beef, and seal. Refrigerate for up to 24 hours.

Strain the beef into a strainer, reserving the marinade. Rest the beef on the counter for 30 minutes. Heat the remaining 1 tablespoon oil in a frying pan over high heat, swirling the pan to coat. Heat until smoke appears, about 2 minutes (the pan needs to be very hot to sear the meat). Add the strained beef and sear, about 2 minutes. Add the reserved marinade until it starts to boil, about 2 minutes. The meat will be medium rare. Transfer to a bowl and garnish with green onion and sesame seeds, if desired. Serve with toothpicks.

SPICY BARBECUED PRAWNS

SERVES 2-4

¾ cup butter
1 tablespoon Spice Blend (recipe at right)
1 pound fresh cold-water prawns (size 26/30)
½ cup heavy cream

Heat the butter in a sauté pan over medium-high heat until melted. Add the spice blend and prawns, searing them on each side until caramelized, about 3 minutes. Add the cream and reduce the sauce until it has a creamy, saucelike consistency. Transfer the prawns to a serving dish, pour the sauce over the top, and serve immediately.

Spice Blend

⅛ cup fine sugar
2 teaspoons cayenne pepper
2 tablespoons paprika
1 tablespoon kosher salt
1 tablespoon garlic powder
1 tablespoon chili powder
1 teaspoon dried rosemary
1 teaspoon dried thyme
1 teaspoon onion powder

Mix all the ingredients together and store in a sealed container until ready to use.

LAKE UNION

Lake Union, carved by a glacier thousands of years ago, connects Lake Washington with Puget Sound, the salty waterway that leads to the vast Pacific Ocean. Many fine restaurants like Daniel's Broiler dot the shores of Lake Union, where a beehive of activity abounds. Floatplanes operated by Kenmore Air use the lake as a runway, shuttling passengers to and from neighboring islands. During summer months, pleasure boats fill the lake, particularly during Seattle's famous Fourth of July fireworks show. The colorful celebration is also viewed from Gas Works, Lake Union's largest park. Remember the "floating homes" in the hit movie *Sleepless in Seattle*? They too are located in Lake Union, on the east and west sides. Other activities on the lake include competitive rowing, canoeing, and various boat shows and festivals.

CHANDLER'S CRABHOUSE

901 Fairview Avenue North, Seattle
(425) 223-2722
WWW.SCHWARTZBROS.COM
Owner: Schwartz Brothers Restaurants

Schwartz Brothers Restaurants, the same elite dining team who owns Daniel's Broiler and Spazzo Italian Grill & Wine Bar, brings you Chandler's Crabhouse. Chandler's opened its doors on beautiful Lake Union in 1988 and showcases what it knows best: crab.

The most popular item on the menu is the locally harvested Dungeness crab, named after a small fishing village on the Strait of Juan de Fuca in Washington State. This crab is sweet, meaty, and a true Pacific Northwest delicacy. Best of all, you can enjoy Dungeness crab throughout the year. Chandler's offers other kinds of crab, too, such as Florida stone crab claws and east coast blue or soft-shelled crab. And there's no shortage of crab recipes on the menu. One of chef Kevin Rohr's favorites is the Dungeness Crab Cake.

"The key to making a great crab cake is to begin the preparation at least a few hours

ahead of time," hints the chef. "This allows the cakes to set up properly. If you try to cook them right away, they'll simply fall apart." Chef Rohr also advises using only fresh crabmeat. "It may be less expensive to use fillers, such as bread or breadcrumbs, but the product won't come close to being as good. A great crab cake should be just that—crab. Chef Rohr suggests a green salad to accompany his crab cakes, such as a Chandler's Seasonal Salad with heirloom tomatoes, cucumbers, and hearts of palm. For a beverage, Chef Rohr suggests a sauvignon blanc, an oaky chardonnay, or a refreshing ice-cold glass of lemonade.

DUNGENESS CRAB CAKES

SERVES 4

2 cups fresh Dungeness crabmeat

2 tablespoons butter

¼ cup chopped red bell pepper

¼ cup diced celery

¼ cup peeled and diced onions

1 tablespoon peeled and minced garlic

½ cup mayonnaise

Salt and pepper to taste

2–3 cups panko (Japanese bread crumbs)

2 tablespoons extra-virgin olive oil

Tartar sauce and fresh lemon slices, for serving

Gently squeeze the crabmeat to remove excess juice.

Melt the butter in a sauté pan over medium heat. Add the bell pepper, celery, onions, and garlic, and lightly sauté for about five minutes. Remove from heat, transfer to a mixing bowl, and allow to cool. Add the crabmeat, mayonnaise, salt, and pepper, and combine.

Next, pour the panko into a shallow baking pan, completely covering the bottom. Shape each ¼ cup or so of crabmeat mixture into a patty and place into the pan. Sprinkle the panko over the top and edges of the cake. Cover the prepared crab cakes with plastic wrap and place in the refrigerator for at least 3 hours to set up.

Add the olive oil to a large sauté pan over medium-high heat. Gently add the cakes and panfry until golden brown and heated through.

Serve immediately with tartar sauce and fresh lemon slices.

THE SEATTLE AQUARIUM

The Seattle Aquarium is a terrific attraction if you'd like to learn more about the local fish and shellfish that come from Pacific Northwest waters. Opened in 1977 at the end of historic Seattle waterfront's Pier 59, the Seattle Aquarium features a variety of displays, including a massive underwater dome that opens a window to such native creatures as salmon, rockfish, halibut, lingcod, skate, and sturgeon. Smaller exhibits showcase various crab—including Dungeness crab—shrimp, scallops, and wolf eels. Yes, the Pacific Ocean off the Washington coast is often dark and frigid, but the abundance of marine life that flourishes below the surface is truly remarkable, including the illusive six-gill shark and the giant Pacific octopus—the largest in the world!

DUNGENESS CRAB & ARTICHOKE DIP
SERVES 4–5

½ cup grated Parmesan cheese
1½ cups mayonnaise
6 ounces (¾ cup) fresh Dungeness crabmeat
4 ounces (½ cup) artichoke hearts, well drained
    and coarsely chopped
Green onion, minced, for garnish
Cayenne pepper, as needed, for garnish
Tortilla chips

In a mixing bowl, combine the cheese, mayonnaise, crabmeat, and artichoke hearts. Blend well with a spoon.

Transfer the crab and artichoke mixture to a small (around 8 x 8-inch) 1½-inch-deep baking dish. Bake at 375°F for 10 minutes, or until brown and heated through.

Garnish with minced green onions and cayenne pepper. Serve warm with tortilla chips.

JOEY—LAKE UNION

9011 FAIRWAY AVENUE NORTH, SEATTLE
(604) 749-JOEY (5639)
WWW.JOEYRESTAURANTS.COM
OWNER: JEFF FULLER

Joey Restaurant (Bellevue, Southcenter, and Lake Union) is a place to see and be seen. It is a chic eatery with a modern flair, where you'll find Microsoft executives discussing corporate strategy during their power lunches and local sports celebrities enjoying the Killer Ahi Tuna Tacos or Spicy Salmon Rolls during their down time.

In the adjacent dining room, Executive Chef Chris Mills wows his fans with delicious food inspired by distinct flavors and cultures found around the world. Chef Mills has received countless accolades and awards for his culinary ingenuity, including scoring an invitation to be a guest chef at the James Beard House in New York City. Additionally, he was one of only two Canadian chefs ever to compete on the original Japanese *Iron Chef* in Tokyo. And not long ago, Chef Mills placed fifth in the world in the Bocuse d'Or culinary competition, while his escapade was captured in a documentary special that aired on the Food Network.

Eager to include a fun bite for this chapter, Chef Mills is proud to share his celebrated Chicken Jalapeño Corn Dogs recipe. This fun appetizer for sharing is a throwback to summer fairs and festivals. The dipping sauce and presentation make these corn dogs a hit at parties.

Chicken Jalapeño Corn Dogs

MAKES 24 BITES

Curry Raisin Mayonnaise:

¼ cup sugar

¼ cup red wine vinegar

¼ cup currants or raisins

1 pinch fresh thyme leaves

1 teaspoon curry powder

1 cup mayonnaise

Squeeze of lemon juice

Black pepper to taste

Corn Dog Batter:

½ cup cornmeal

½ cup all-purpose flour

1 teaspoon salt

½ teaspoon baking soda

Cayenne pepper to taste

½ cup cream-style corn

1 cup buttermilk

¼ cup minced white onion

1 jalapeño, seeded and minced

Corn Dogs:

24 6-inch bamboo skewers

3 boneless breasts of chicken, cut into ¾-inch dice
   (24 pieces)

Cornstarch for coating

Oil in a home fryer (or shallow wok)

To make the mayonnaise: In a small saucepan combine the sugar and vinegar over medium heat until the mixture reduces to a light syrup. Add the currants or raisins, thyme, and curry powder. Stir well and remove from heat, allowing the mixture to cool and steep for 15 minutes. Once cool, add the mayonnaise, lemon juice, and pepper, then transfer to a container suitable for the refrigerator. Store up to 5 days.

To make the corn dog batter: In a mixing bowl combine the cornmeal, flour, salt, baking soda, and cayenne pepper. In another bowl combine the corn, buttermilk, onions, and jalapeño. Whisk the buttermilk "wet" ingredients into the cornmeal "dry" ingredients, just enough to bring them together as a batter. The batter should be slightly thicker than pancake batter.

To make the corn dogs: Preheat fryer to 350°F. Skewer one piece of chicken per bamboo skewer. Dredge each piece of skewered chicken in cornstarch, then dip the chicken into the corn dog batter until thoroughly coated. Carefully submerge each piece of chicken into the hot oil of the fryer, holding the skewer end to fry each battered piece into a ball. (Use caution: The oil is extremely hot!) Once the exterior of the chicken is cooking, the entire skewer may be carefully dropped into the oil. Cook for 2 to 3 minutes, maintaining the temperature of the fryer to control the color. Remove one piece of chicken and cut into the center to ensure it is cooked through. Remove the skewered chicken from the oil with a slotted spoon and drain. Serve warm with a side of Curry Raisin Mayonnaise.

PURPLE CAFÉ AND WINE BAR

1225 4TH AVENUE, SEATTLE
(206) 829-2280
WWW.THEPURPLECAFE.COM
OWNERS: LARRY AND TABITHA KUROFSKY

If you're looking for a casual eating experience with plenty of elbow room, perfectly made cocktails, and superior service, look no further than the Purple Café and Wine Bar in downtown Seattle. Upon entering the casual, inviting establishment, you encounter the horseshoe-shaped bar right in the middle of the restaurant, accentuated by a massive wine tower housing five thousand bottles and stretching more than twenty feet in the air to the ceiling. The food—American style with seasonal Northwest ingredients—is just as inviting, which is why Purple is a culinary hit regardless of what mood you're in.

"Purple Café and Wine Bar merges casual sophistication with an upbeat metropolitan style," describes owner Larry Kurofsky. The restaurant has also been a hit with the locals, and *Seattle Met* magazine adds: "There's nothing like it downtown . . . and they won't let you down."

The first Purple Café and Wine Bar opened in 2001 in Woodinville (now a Washington wine-tasting destination on the other side of town) by Larry and Tabitha Kurofsky. Today, four thriving locations serve Seattle and the Eastside. The restaurant also features a global wine menu, which includes ninety selections by the glass and more than six hundred by the bottle. The restaurant is truly a food- and wine-pairing experience, as almost half the menu includes suggested pairings such as the cheeses and tapas-style small bites featured in the bar. One of those popular small bites—a baked brie served with apricot preserves, caramelized onions, candied walnuts, grapes, and house-made crackers—is showcased here.

BAKED BRIE WITH CANDIED WALNUTS & CARAMELIZED ONIONS

SERVES 2-4

1 tablespoon vegetable oil

1 small white or yellow onion, very thinly sliced

Pinch of kosher salt

4 sheets phyllo dough

6 tablespoons clarified butter, melted

1 (4–8-ounce) wheel ripe brie cheese

1½–2 tablespoons apricot jam

3–4 tablespoons Candied Walnuts (recipe next page)

Fresh fruit of your choice, such as red grapes, apple slices, or pear slices

Baguette slices or crackers

Heat the oil in a medium skillet over medium heat. When the oil is hot, add the onions and salt and cook, stirring occasionally, until the onions are tender and golden, about 25 to 30 minutes. Adjust the heat if necessary so the onions don't brown too quickly or burn. Set aside.

While the onions are cooking, arrange the oven rack in the center of the oven. Spray a baking sheet with nonstick cooking spray or line with parchment paper.

Lay the phyllo dough on a clean, damp kitchen towel on a dry work surface and cover with another damp kitchen towel. Lay a sheet of dough on the baking sheet and brush lightly with melted butter.

Place a second piece of dough across the first piece of dough to form a cross shape and brush lightly with butter. Place a third piece of dough diagonally over the cross and brush lightly with butter. Place the fourth piece of dough diagonally over the third piece of dough (to form an X shape) and brush lightly with butter.

Cut the brie horizontally through the middle to form a top and bottom layer. Place the bottom layer of brie in the center of the phyllo dough. Brush with apricot jam, and then arrange the onions and the Candied Walnuts evenly over the jam. Cover with the top layer of brie. Form a beggar's purse by gathering all eight ends of the phyllo dough, bringing them together over the top of the brie and pinching them together until the brie is totally encased in dough. Brush lightly with butter, then place the phyllo package in the refrigerator for 30 minutes to 1 hour before proceeding to the next step.

Preheat the oven to 450°F. Cover the brie loosely with aluminum foil and place in the oven for 5 minutes. Remove the foil and continue baking for 1 to 2 minutes, or until the phyllo turns golden in color. Remove the brie from the oven and transfer to a serving plate. Arrange the fresh fruit and baguette slices or crackers around the cheese and serve immediately.

CANDIED WALNUTS

1 large egg white
1 cup whole walnuts
¼ cup sugar
2 tablespoons firmly packed brown sugar
½ teaspoon pure vanilla extract

Preheat oven to 300°F. Line a rimmed baking sheet with aluminum foil or parchment paper and spray with nonstick cooking spray.

In a small mixing bowl, whisk the egg white until light and frothy. Add the walnuts and mix well. Sprinkle the nuts with granulated and brown sugar, add the vanilla, and stir until the walnuts are evenly coated with sugar. Arrange the walnuts in a single layer on the baking sheet without crowding and cook for 5 minutes. Remove the nuts from the oven and stir. Continue cooking, stirring the nuts every 5 minutes, for a total of 25 to 30 minutes of cooking time, or until the walnuts no longer look moist and are medium caramel in color.

Remove nuts from the oven and transfer the baking sheet to a wire rack. When cool enough to handle, break apart the nuts, then dry completely on the baking sheet on the wire rack. Store in an airtight container at room temperature until ready to serve.

SEAFOOD STARTERS, SOUPS & SALADS

It doesn't seem to matter what season it is in Seattle, because fresh seafood, soups, and salads are always on the menu.

Atop Seattle's iconic Space Needle, hearty dishes such as sizzling razor clam fritters and lentil soup with smoky bacon reflect true Pacific Northwest fare, as do the Penn Cove mussels and Dungeness crab and corn chowder served at Ray's Boathouse. Emmer & Rye is proud of its local mussels steamed in a savory vegetable broth as well as its pear and celeriac soup with leeks. Step into Woodinville wine country and Barking Frog will dazzle you with its hazelnut-dusted sea scallops and golden delicious butternut squash soup, or zip across Lake Washington to Capital Hill for another mussel variation and a hot bowl of coriander potato soup. With many cold, damp days in Seattle, soup is never far from the menu. Volterra has an interesting "oil" soup, and guests at the Salish Lodge can spoon its chestnut-apple soup while taking in the breathtaking sights of famous Snoqualmie Falls.

Because salads seem to go hand in hand with soups, Salish Lodge kicks it off with a roasted beet salad, and James Beard Award–winner Maria Hines of Tilth unveils her winter root vegetable salad. Salty's Restaurant plates its favorite fennel pollen honey-glazed salmon salad, and Bastille in historic Ballard wraps up this chapter by inviting home cooks to try both hot and cold: a warm cabbage salad and a chilled arugula and beet salad with a tangy pistachio vinaigrette.

SkyCity at the Needle

400 Broad Street, Seattle
(206) 905-2100
www.spaceneedle.com/restaurant/
Owner: Space Needle Corporation

If you're looking for a restaurant with quintessential views of Seattle, look no farther than SkyCity atop the iconic Space Needle. Built in 1962, the Space Needle was erected for the World's Fair. Today the monument serves as a symbol of the Emerald City. Dining inside the monument is also quite the adventure.

Begin your culinary journey by stepping into an elevator and rising five hundred feet in the air to the SkyCity entrance. Once inside, the circular restaurant revolving beneath your feet offers expansive views as you prepare to feast on fresh, delicious Northwest fare. Executive Chef and Seattle native Jeff Maxfield is a strong supporter of using local seafood on his menus, such as salmon, clams, and crab. He also uses Northwest-grown beef and fruits and vegetables from nearby farms.

One dish Chef Maxfield enjoys—but did not create—is the famous Lunar Orbiter. It's the only item remaining from the original menu when the restaurant first opened its doors. Part spectacle, part dessert, the Lunar Orbiter is SkyCity's version of an ice cream sundae, but with a twist. When the dish arrives tableside, a large cloud of steam (courtesy of dry ice) spills over the table, as if the molten spacecraft just touched down from another planet. It's definitely an out-of-this-world sight—and taste—to experience.

Razor Clam Fritters with Herb Rémoulade

SERVES 4–6

1½ cups flour

1½ teaspoons baking powder

1 egg, beaten

1 cup milk

2 tablespoons finely chopped fresh flat-leaf parsley

2 tablespoons finely chopped fresh thyme

2 tablespoons finely chopped fresh chives

1 pound razor clams, cleaned and chopped

Salt and pepper to taste

Vegetable oil for frying

In a mixing bowl, sift together the flour and baking powder. Add the egg and milk and mix thoroughly until smooth. Add the herbs and chopped clams and season with salt and pepper.

In a deep fryer or pot, heat the vegetable oil to 340°F (check temperature using a candy thermometer). Scoop 1-ounce portions of the fritter mixture, carefully place into the hot oil, and cook until golden brown. Remove the fritters from the oil and drain on paper towels. Serve immediately with herb rémoulade.

Herb Rémoulade

1 medium yellow onion, peeled and diced

2 dill pickles, chopped

6 fresh basil leaves, chopped

2 tablespoons chopped fresh baby dill

1 cup mayonnaise

1 tablespoon lemon juice

2 tablespoons capers

2 tablespoons Dijon mustard

¼ teaspoon Tapatio or other hot sauce

Salt and pepper to taste

In a food processor, puree the onions, pickles, and fresh herbs. Transfer to a medium mixing bowl.

Add the mayonnaise, lemon juice, capers, mustard, and hot sauce. Mix well. Season with salt and pepper.

Palouse Lentil Soup with Smoky Bacon, Roasted Grapes & Sorrel

MAKES 1 GALLON

Lentil Soup:

1½ pounds sliced bacon

1½ pounds onion, cut into small dice

1½ pounds carrots, cut into small dice

4 ounces (6–8 large cloves) chopped garlic

1½ pounds dried lentils

2 bay leaves

1 cinnamon stick

1 gallon (16 cups) low-sodium chicken broth

Salt and pepper, to taste

Garnish:

1 bunch (about 2–3 cups) red seedless grapes

1 tablespoon olive oil

Sorrel, thinly sliced, as needed

Mint, thinly sliced, as needed

For the soup: In a stainless steel stockpot over medium heat, render the bacon until slightly crispy. Add the onions, carrots, and garlic, and cook until the vegetables are translucent. Add the lentils and cook until evenly coated with bacon fat. Add the bay leaves, cinnamon stick, and chicken broth and bring to a simmer. Cook until the lentils are tender, approximately 20 minutes. Season with salt and pepper.

For the garnish: Preheat the oven to 400°F. Toss the grapes in the olive oil and place on a cookie sheet. Bake in the preheated oven for 5 minutes, or until the skins split.

Transfer the soup to serving bowls and garnish with sorrel, mint, and roasted red grapes.

THE SPACE NEEDLE

The Space Needle stands as a historic landmark of the Pacific Northwest region. Towering above Seattle, the 605-foot-high structure is windproof, earthquake-proof, and lightning-proof. An observation deck is located near the top, where the rotating SkyCity restaurant welcomes guests—after their one minute elevator ride—to a gastronomic delight above the city. On a clear day from atop the Needle, visitors can marvel at the snow-capped peaks of the Cascade and Olympic Mountains, Mount Rainier, and Mount Baker. They can also see neighboring islands near and far. At the time it was built in 1962, the Space Needle was the tallest building west of the Mississippi River. Today other Seattle structures, like the Columbia Center, soar higher than the Needle, standing more than 900 feet tall.

Ray's Boathouse

6049 Seaview Avenue Northwest, Seattle
(206) 789-3770
www.rays.com
Owners: Elizabeth Gingrich, Russ Wohlers, Earl Lasher,
and Jack Sikma

Whether it includes sitting on a deck overlooking Lake Washington or peering out a window to marvel at Puget Sound and the beautiful inland waterway, waterfront dining is very popular in Seattle. Ray's Boathouse, which has been serving up some of the best seafood in the city since 1973, is one of those restaurants where picturesque views are perfectly complemented with exceptional cuisine.

The restaurant, once a fish-n-chips cafe, offers sweeping views of the shimmering sea while Executive Chef Peter Birk impresses guests with fresh, local fish and shellfish combinations such as Grilled Neah Bay Chinook Salmon, Chatham Strait Sablefish, Penn Cove Mussels, and, of course, Dungeness Crab—always a hit with Seattleites.

The same mouthwatering seafood is served in the bar and pairs well with generously poured signature cocktails or a fine glass of Northwest wine from the lengthy menu. Seating is limited in the bar, so make sure you arrive early or hang out by the counter, especially during happy hour. If you want one of the sought-after tables that overlook the sea, it's definitely worth the wait.

Penn Cove Mussels in Thai Coconut Curry Broth

SERVES 4

1 cup coconut milk

2 teaspoons fresh lime juice

1 teaspoon red curry paste

2 teaspoons Thai fish sauce

$2/3$ cup sake

1 teaspoon minced garlic

1 teaspoon minced fresh ginger

1 teaspoon chopped fresh basil

2 pounds Penn Cove mussels, cleaned and debearded

2–4 sprigs fresh basil

In a large bowl, whisk together the coconut milk, lime juice, curry paste, fish sauce, sake, garlic, ginger, and basil.

Heat a heavy saucepan over high heat for about 30 seconds. Add the mussels and coconut milk broth. Bring to a boil and reduce heat. Cover and simmer until mussels fully open, about 5 minutes.

Divide mussels into bowls, garnish with sprigs of basil, and serve with coconut milk broth and plenty of crusty bread.

To ensure the safety and quality of the shellfish, make sure mussels are alive and shells are closed. Always purchase from a reputable fishmonger. After cooking, discard any unopened mussels.

Ray's Dungeness Crab & Corn Chowder

SERVES UP TO 10 AS A MAIN COURSE

½ cup butter

1 cup diced onion

1 cup diced red bell pepper

1 cup diced green bell pepper

½ cup all-purpose flour

½ gallon milk

4 cups corn kernels (fresh or frozen, uncooked)

3 cups diced red potatoes, skin on

1 teaspoon dried thyme

2 teaspoons salt

1½ teaspoons ground black pepper

12 ounces Dungeness crabmeat

1 cup cream

2 tablespoons chopped chives

Melt the butter in a 5-quart stockpot over medium-high heat. Add the onions and sauté until translucent. Add the red and green peppers. Mix in the flour and stir to make a roux.

Stir in the milk, corn, potatoes, and thyme and bring to a boil. Add salt and pepper to taste. Reduce the heat and simmer until potatoes are soft, stirring occasionally, approximately 15 to 20 minutes. Add the crabmeat and cream. Garnish with chopped chives.

Emmer & Rye

1825 Queen Anne Avenue North, Seattle
(206) 282-0680
www.emmerandrye.com
Owner: Seth Caswell

The charming Queen Anne neighborhood, off I-5 via the Mercer Street exit, is ranked one of the best Seattle neighborhoods by *Seattle* magazine. Queen Anne is also home to some of the best restaurants in the city, one of those being Emmer & Rye.

In 2005, Chef Seth Caswell, who spent years cooking for New York's elite, packed his bags and arrived in Seattle, where his next culinary adventures began. Five years later he opened Emmer & Rye. Familiar with the fresh, high-quality, and sustainable foods of the region and a strong advocate of supporting the local community, Chef Caswell set out to create a menu that would showcase the best local foods he could find. "I've always been enamored with the variety of ingredients in the Pacific Northwest," says the chef. "This encourages me to get creative with the ingredients." Today not only are his dishes creative, but they reflect those who provide the foods, from farmers to fishermen.

The two recipes featured here give homage to local Northwest foods and their respective seasons. The mussels, especially the summer varieties cultivated in nearby Puget Sound, are perfect accompaniments for the summer's brief but flavorful bounty of vegetables like tomatoes, corn, and basil. And, with the hearty pear and celery root perfectly complementing the crispy leek threads, the soup is just right for a cold winter day.

Mussels with Summer Vegetable Broth

SERVES 4 AS AN APPETIZER OR 2 AS AN ENTREE

2 pounds mussels, cleaned
2 teaspoons olive oil
2 garlic cloves, peeled and slivered
1 shallot bulb, peeled and sliced (you can
    also use red onion)
1 ear grilled corn, shucked
1 small green zucchini, sliced
2 large beefsteak tomatoes, diced
6 sprigs fresh basil, chopped
Kosher salt and freshly ground black pepper to taste
½ cup white wine
2 tablespoons unsalted butter

Clean the mussels well by scrubbing the shells and removing the byssus or "beard" with a gentle tug. Transfer the mussels to a colander and run under very cold water. Use the mussels immediately or cover them with a damp towel and refrigerate in the colander with some ice.

Heat a large sauté pan over medium heat and add the olive oil. Add the garlic and shallots and begin to soften, but do not brown. Add the corn, zucchini, tomatoes, and basil and season with salt and pepper. Sauté for 2 minutes, or until the vegetables begin to soften and the tomatoes release their juices. Add the white wine and bring to a boil.

Add the mussels to the hot mixture and toss to cover the shells with broth. Cover and turn heat to high. Occasionally shake the pan (keep covered) and, after 3 minutes, add the butter. Cover and cook an additional 2 minutes. Taste for seasoning and adjust accordingly.

Transfer the mussels to a large serving bowl and serve. Make sure you have lots of bread on hand to soak up the juices.

Pear & Celeriac Soup with Crispy Leeks

SERVES 6

Pear & Celeriac Soup:

2 tablespoons unsalted butter

2 leeks, some greens removed and chopped

2 pounds celeriac, peeled and roughly chopped
   into large pieces

1 quart vegetable stock

1 pound Bartlett or Anjou pears, peeled,
   cored, and chopped

1 tablespoon heavy cream

1 tablespoon kosher salt

½ teaspoon freshly ground white pepper

Crispy Leeks:

2 cups grape-seed oil

2 leeks, whites julienned

Kosher salt and freshly ground black pepper
   to taste

To make the soup: Melt the butter in a heavy-bottomed saucepan with high sides. Add the leeks and stir over low heat for 5 minutes, until the leeks are softened. Add the celeriac and vegetable stock, bring to a boil, reduce the heat, then simmer for 20 minutes. Add the pears during the final 4 minutes of cooking. When the celeriac and pears are mushy, transfer everything to a blender and carefully puree for 2 minutes. Add the cream, salt, and white pepper to taste, then blend the soup well.

To make the crispy leeks: Heat the grape-seed oil to 375°F. In small batches, carefully drop the julienned leeks into the hot oil. Stir for 15 seconds. Remove the leeks with a slotted spoon and transfer to paper towels to drain. Immediately sprinkle lightly with salt and pepper.

To serve: Ladle about ¾ cup of soup into each serving bowl. Gather a pile of crispy leeks and place in the center of each serving.

BARKING FROG

14580 NORTHEAST 145TH STREET, WOODINVILLE
(425) 424-2999
WWW.WILLOWSLODGE.COM
OWNER: PREFERRED HOTEL GROUP

A pastoral suburb outside of Seattle, Woodinville has become the heart of a burgeoning local wine industry. With alluring tasting rooms and restaurants combined with fun outdoor activities such as movie nights and live concerts, Woodinville's many offerings present the makings of a fantastic day and evening.

Across the street from the famed Chateau St. Michelle Winery is the Willows Lodge—a haven for locals and out-of-town guests. For those looking for a delicious meal, whether breakfast, brunch, lunch, or dinner, Barking Frog inside the Willows is the restaurant of choice. Led by Chef Bobby Moore, Barking Frog specializes in fresh, local fare paired with—of course—exemplary wines that have won the praises of *Wine Spectator*'s Award of Excellence.

Chef Moore enjoys using sweet and savory ingredients together. He selected two of his favorite recipes to share with the home cook—Hazelnut-Dusted Sea Scallops with Creamy Polenta & Vanilla Drizzle, and Butternut Squash Soup. "The hazelnut-dusted scallops are a signature dish for Barking Frog and have been well received by a variety of our guests," he says. The dish pairs nicely with a great Oregon pinot or Northwest white wine. "The Butternut Squash Soup is more traditional with the addition of some heat from jalapeños and sweetness from vanilla bean." And for the perfect wine accompaniment, Chef Moore suggests a nice Northwest sauvignon blanc.

HAZELNUT-DUSTED SEA SCALLOPS WITH CREAMY POLENTA & VANILLA DRIZZLE

SERVES 4

8 cups whole milk

2 cups polenta

1 cup honey

1 vanilla bean

16 fresh sea scallops

2 cups hazelnut meal (available in fine grocery stores and online)

Salt and pepper to taste

¼ cup clarified butter

¾ cup hazelnuts, blanched, roasted, and ground

Baby spinach or baby carrots, for serving

Combine the milk and polenta in a saucepan. Cook on low heat until the polenta thickens. Cover and set aside.

Pour the honey into another saucepan. Split the vanilla bean and add it to the honey. Heat over low until the vanilla bean has released its flavor into the honey. Taste to check. Set aside.

Preheat the oven to 500°F.

Dust the scallops with the hazelnut meal, salt, and pepper. Heat the clarified butter in a large ovenproof sauté pan over high heat. When hot, add the scallops without crowding. Sear on one side for about 20 seconds, then immediately transfer the pan to the oven and cook for 3 minutes.

Remove the pan from the oven, turn the scallops over, and allow them to continue cooking until medium rare.

To serve: Divide the scallops among four individual plates. Place ½ cup of cooked polenta on each serving plate. Drizzle the vanilla-honey sauce around the plate and sprinkle with ground hazelnuts. Serve with a side of baby spinach or baby carrots.

BUTTERNUT SQUASH SOUP

SERVES 10

1 large butternut squash, peeled, split, and seeded
  (or enough to cover ½ cookie sheet)
¼ cup melted butter
1 cup sherry wine, divided
3 carrots, peeled and chopped
Cold water
3 celery stalks, chopped
1 medium onion, peeled and chopped
½ tablespoon chili flakes
½ jalapeño, stemmed and split
½ bunch fresh thyme
1 tablespoon crushed black peppercorns,
  crushed
2 bay leaves
⅛ cup (2–3 cloves) garlic, peeled and
  poached in boiling water to soften
1 vanilla bean
Crème fraîche to taste
Salt and white pepper to taste

Line a cookie sheet with parchment paper. Peel, split, and seed enough butternut squash to cover half the pan. Brush the squash with the melted butter and roast under the broiler until edges have a medium-dark caramelization. Remove the squash and deglaze with ½ cup of the sherry. Return squash to the oven and continue to roast until nearly dry. Remove from oven and set aside.

Place the carrots in a large sauté pan over medium heat and lightly brown. Deglaze with a little water and add the celery and onion. Continue sautéing until the celery and onion are lightly caramelized. Add the remaining ½ cup sherry and deglaze, bringing the liquid to a full boil.

Place the chili flakes, jalapeño, thyme, peppercorns, and bay leaves in a small piece of cheesecloth. Fold the cheesecloth and tie with kitchen string, creating a sachet.

Add the sachet of spices to the sauté pan. Then add the roasted squash and softened garlic. Split and scrape the vanilla bean into the pan. Add 4 cups of cold water. Lower heat and simmer until the squash is soft and tender, about 10 minutes.

Remove the sachet and vanilla bean. Transfer the squash mixture to a large blender and blend until smooth. Strain the soup into a large bowl, then add crème fraîche and season with salt and white pepper. Serve warm.

Poppy

622 BROADWAY EAST, SEATTLE
(206) 324-1108
WWW.POPPYSEATTLE.COM
OWNER: JERRY TRAUNFELD

One of the more unique restaurants you'll find in Seattle is Poppy, the brainchild of James Beard Award–winning Chef Jerry Traunfeld. Formerly the executive chef at Washington State's acclaimed the Herbfarm and the Seattle Alexis Hotel, Chef Traunfeld has created an innovative dining experience.

Housed in a 1920s art deco storefront in Seattle's lively Capitol Hill neighborhood, Poppy's Scandinavian-inspired interior and modern design make for a stylish setting to enjoy the colorful foods and drinks. There's also outdoor seating on the sidewalk and in the herb garden courtyard when the weather permits.

Guests at Poppy—named after Chef Traunfeld's mother—will raise eyebrows when they find seven- and ten-item *thalis* on the menu. And just what are thalis? They are an assortment of varying dishes assembled on one platter, named after the Indian-style culinary experience. Inspired by local foods of the Northwest, typical thali dishes you might find are wild-caught king salmon, grilled Waygu beef, red-pepper apricot soup, watermelon and cucumber salad, golden beets, corn and basil spoon bread, plum-shiso pickles, and nigella-poppy naan. The savory meals can be enjoyed in the dining room or in the lively bar, which offers a popular happy hour that includes exotic cocktails with fun names like Block Party, Turkish Delight, Loveless, and the Snap.

Panfried Mussels with Lovage Aioli

SERVES 4–6

2 pounds medium to large fresh mussels,
  cleaned and debearded
½ cup dry white wine
1 cup all-purpose flour
1 teaspoon fine sea salt
½ teaspoon freshly ground black pepper
Olive oil for frying
Lovage Aioli (recipe below)
Chopped lovage (or dill) for serving

Place the cleaned and debearded mussels in a large pot. Pour the wine over them, cover the pot, and cook over high heat until the mussels open, and then for 1 additional minute after that. Drain the mussels in a colander (discarding any unopened mussels), spread them on a baking sheet, and then refrigerate until cool. When cool, remove the meat from the shells, using a paring knife to aid if they cling. Clean and wash half the shells and reserve.

Next, mix the flour with the salt and pepper on a large plate. Pour a ¼-inch layer of olive oil into a large skillet placed over medium heat. Dredge half the mussels with the seasoned flour and shake off excess flour. Carefully add the mussels to the pan in a single layer. The mussels may "sputter and pop," so use a splatter screen, if you have one. Cook the mussels until lightly browned on both sides. Drain the mussels on paper towels and repeat with the second batch. Sprinkle lightly with more salt, if needed.

Arrange the mussels in the reserved shells and top each with a dollop of aioli and a sprinkle of chopped lovage.

Lovage Aioli

MAKES 1½ CUPS

2 large egg yolks
2 tablespoons freshly squeezed lemon juice
2 cloves garlic
½ teaspoon kosher salt
1 dash Tabasco sauce
¼ cup lovage leaves (substitute dill if lovage
  is not available)
1 cup extra-virgin olive oil

Combine the egg yolks, lemon juice, garlic, salt, Tabasco, and lovage leaves in a food processor. Turn the machine on and slowly pour in the olive oil in a steady stream.

Serve the aioli atop panfried mussels or on the side as a dipping sauce. Use the extra aioli in sandwiches or salads.

Coriander Potato Soup

SERVES 8

2 tablespoons vegetable oil, such as peanut or canola

2 medium-size leeks, white and light green part only, washed and chopped

4 cloves garlic, peeled and chopped

1 tablespoon chopped fresh ginger

6 cups water

1 pound Yukon gold potatoes, peeled and diced

1½ tablespoons coriander seed

3 strips orange zest, removed with a vegetable peeler

1 cup half-and-half

1 cup whole milk plain yogurt

2 teaspoons kosher salt and freshly ground black pepper

Coarsely chopped cilantro for garnish

Pour the oil into a large saucepan over medium heat. Add the leeks, garlic, and ginger. Cook, stirring often, until the leek is wilted and softened but not browned, about 5 minutes. Add the water and potatoes. When the liquid comes to a simmer, cover the pan, lower the heat, and cook until the potatoes are very soft, 20 to 30 minutes.

While the soup is simmering, put the coriander seed and orange zest in a small saucepan. Toss over medium heat until the seeds smell strongly toasty and the color is a few shades darker. Pour the seed and zest onto a paper towel to cool. When cool, grind in a rotary coffee mill.

Add the toasted coriander-orange mixture to the soup and simmer for an additional 5 minutes. Remove from heat and stir in the half-and-half and yogurt. Puree the soup in two batches in a blender just until smooth. Return the soup to the saucepan and season with salt and pepper. Garnish with chopped cilantro and serve.

The soup may also be served chilled.

Volterra

5411 Ballard Avenue Northwest, Seattle
(206) 789-5100
www.volterrarestaurant.com
Owners: Don Curtiss and Michelle Quisenberry

The list of celebrity and critic praise is endless. Celebrity chef Rachael Ray admits: "It's one of my favorite restaurants in the world." *Wine Spectator* acknowledges: "One of America's most innovative chefs." So what are they referencing? They're talking about Volterra, a restaurant situated in the heart of Seattle named after a central town in Tuscany, which serves traditional Italian cuisine in a casual and contemporary Tuscan setting to anyone craving all things Italian.

Situated in the Historic Ballard district, which is better known for commercial fishing fleets and famous crabbing boats (as seen on the Discovery Channel's *Deadliest Catch*)

than world-class eateries, Volterra has found its niche amid the salty dogs. From the moment you step inside, the harmonious blend of Washington State and Italy embraces you, from the crystal chandeliers and softly lit sconces, to the black-and-white photographs and red wine walls. But it is Chef Don Curtiss's menu that is the premier attraction.

"Like Tuscany, we at Volterra like to communicate through food," says Chef Curtiss, who opened the restaurant in 2005 with wife Michelle Quisenberry. "And that begins by using the highest-quality ingredients prepared simply."

Whether you order the Baked Gnocchi with Wild Boar Sausage, the Braised Pork Cheeks, the Tuscan Limoncello Rosemary Drop Cocktail, or a wonderful glass of Tuscan wine, Chef Curtiss and Michelle want you to feel like you're coming home for dinner, and that's exactly how you'll feel when you visit Volterra.

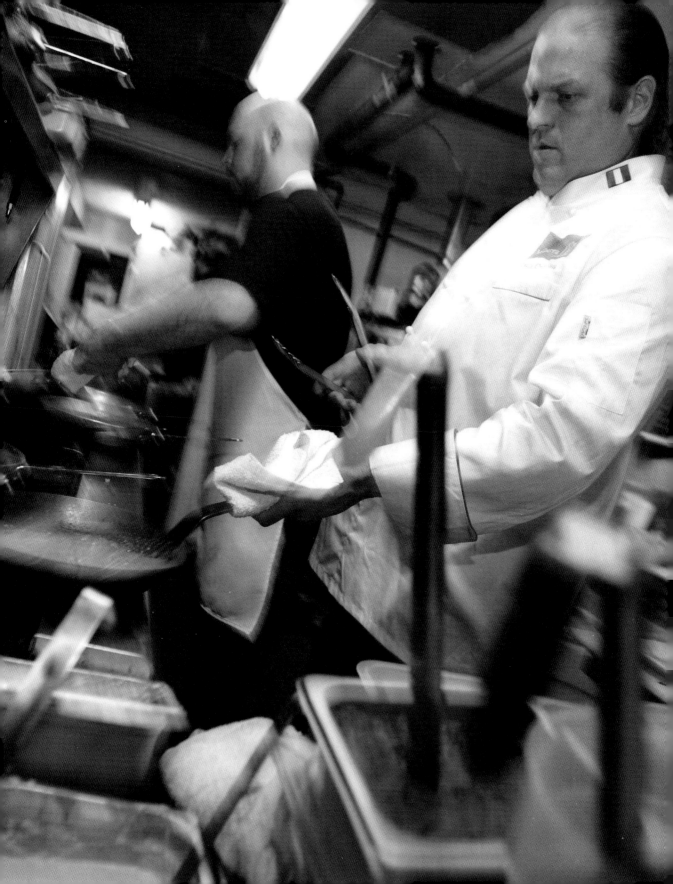

OIL SOUP

SERVES 6–8

Soup:

4 tablespoons olive oil

4 ounces pancetta

1 cup peeled and diced onions

1 tablespoon chopped fresh sage

1 tablespoon chopped fresh rosemary

Salt and black pepper to taste

3 small cans (15 ounces each) Italian cannellini
beans, well drained

6 cups chicken stock

Croutons:

2 cups cubed (¼-inch pieces) bread

2 tablespoons olive oil

Salt and black pepper to taste

Garnish:

Olive oil, for drizzling

Fresh chives, minced fine

For the soup: In a medium stockpot, heat the olive oil until hot. Add the pancetta and crisp slowly until golden brown.

Add the onions, sage, rosemary, salt, and pepper and cook, stirring frequently, until the onions are translucent and starting to turn brown.

Add the cannellini beans and chicken stock. Simmer the soup for 20 to 30 minutes and then puree with a wand mixer or blender until smooth.

For the croutons: Preheat the oven to 400°F. Toss the bread cubes with the olive oil and salt and pepper and spread out on a cookie sheet. Bake until golden brown and slightly crisp, about 8 minutes.

To serve: Ladle the soup into serving bowls. Sprinkle with croutons, drizzle with a generous amount of olive oil, and sprinkle with chives.

Polenta Custard with Wild Mushrooms

SERVES 6–8

Custard:

6 cups water

2 cups whole milk

Salt and black pepper to taste

2 cups fine cornmeal

2 sticks unsalted butter

1 cup grated Parmesan cheese

Butter for lining custard cups

8–10 (1-inch) cubes Fontina cheese

Sauce:

2 tablespoons olive oil

1 pound local wild mushrooms,
    cleaned and sliced

Salt and black pepper, as needed

½ cup Marsala wine

2 cups demi-glace

2 tablespoons unsalted butter

White truffle oil, as needed

For the custard: In a medium saucepan, combine the water, milk, salt, and pepper and bring to a boil. Slowly whisk in the cornmeal and continue to stir until the polenta starts to cook and becomes one entity. Simmer the polenta until it is cooked and smooth and thick. Add the butter and Parmesan and whisk in thoroughly until the butter is melted and the cheese is incorporated.

Butter the insides of 8 to 10 6-ounce custard cups. Fill the buttered custard cups with polenta, then place a piece of Fontina cheese in the center of each and push it down until it is completely covered with polenta. Let cool and set aside.

For the sauce: In a small saucepan over medium heat, heat the olive oil and then add the mushrooms, salt, and pepper and cook until the mushrooms are soft and starting to turn golden brown. Add the Marsala and reduce a little. Add the demi-glace and reduce until the sauce becomes thickened. Then melt in the butter.

To serve: Heat the custards in a 450°F oven until hot and the cheese is melted in the center. Transfer to a serving plate and top with sauce. Drizzle with white truffle oil and serve immediately.

THE DINING ROOM AT SALISH LODGE & SPA

6501 RAILROAD AVENUE, SNOQUALMIE
(425) 888-2556
WWW.SALISHLODGE.COM
OWNER: THE MUCKLESHOOT TRIBE

There are many fabulous views in Seattle, but one that is definitely worth the drive is heading east on I-90 to dine at Salish Lodge & Spa, which overlooks the plunging Snoqualmie Falls. Cascading more than three hundred feet into the icy river below, the falls are a remarkable sight. Equally impressive is Salish Lodge, an eighty-nine room retreat built on a rocky perch that provides optimal viewing of the falls.

Dining at Salish Lodge is highly recommended, and the food is remarkable. Relying on the area's fresh local ingredients, Executive Chef Chuck Courtney takes pride in combining authentic Northwest flavors with his personal creative flare. The result is memorable dishes like the two showcased here. "The rich, warm Chestnut-Apple Soup highlights the crisp Wenatchee apples from eastern Washington and is effortless to prepare while remaining refined," explains Chef Courtney. "Drizzled with homemade Cranberry-Walnut Vinaigrette, the Roasted Beet Salad is an accessible, subtly sophisticated dish created with locally sourced beets and Rogue River Blue Cheese from Oregon." Enjoy the hearty flavors of these two featured dishes bursting with easy-to-find, farm-fresh ingredients available to share with friends, family, and loved ones for evening supper or a delightful dinner party.

For those who happen to dine at Salish Lodge, make sure to take a stroll to the observatory deck, which is just a stone's throw from the lodge entrance. Seeing Snoqualmie Falls up close is a sight not to be missed.

Chestnut-Apple Soup

SERVES 4

2 tablespoons butter

½ cup peeled and diced yellow onions

1 tablespoon peeled and minced shallots

2 cloves garlic, peeled and chopped

1 pound peeled chestnuts

4 cups peeled and diced Fuji apples

½ cup brandy

½ cup Madeira wine

2 stems thyme

2 bay leaves

½ teaspoon white peppercorns

3 quarts (12 cups) chicken stock, heated

1 pint heavy cream

Salt and white pepper to taste

Optional Garnishes:

Roasted chestnuts

Sour cream

Toasted pumpkin seeds

Apple chips

Place the butter in a stockpot over low heat and melt gently. Add the onions and shallots and cook (sweat) for 5 minutes without browning. Add the garlic, chestnuts, and apples; sweat briefly. Deglaze with the brandy and Madeira and bring to a boil.

Meanwhile, place the thyme stems, bay leaves, and peppercorns in a small piece of cheesecloth. Fold the cheesecloth and tie with kitchen string, creating an herb sachet.

Simmer the stockpot contents to reduce by half and add the heated chicken stock and herb sachet. Bring back to a simmer and cook gently for 30 to 45 minutes, or until chestnuts are soft. Transfer to a blender, then blend and season to taste.

Add the cream, blend again, and strain into serving bowls.

Garnish soup with bits of roasted chestnuts, a dollop of sour cream, toasted pumpkin seeds, or crunched apple chips.

SNOQUALMIE FALLS

Snoqualmie Falls is a massive waterfall located on the Snoqualmie River and is one of the area's popular scenic attractions. Featured in the hit television series *Twin Peaks,* the almost 300-foot waterfall is a natural landmark that attracts more than one million visitors a year. Overlooking the picturesque falls is the Salish Lodge & Spa (formerly known as the Snoqualmie Falls Lodge). The lodge was first built in 1919 and welcomed visitors traveling to see the falls. The lodge reopened under the new name in 1988, boasting eighty-nine rooms, a spa, and exquisite dining. The fireplace is the only remaining structure of the original lodge.

ROASTED BEET SALAD

SERVES 4

2 medium-size red beets

Olive oil, as needed

½ cup julienned Bartlett pears (approximately
    1 or 2 pears)

½ cup julienned Belgian endive (approximately
    1 or 2 heads)

¼ cup peeled and minced shallots (approximately
    1 or 2 shallots)

½ cup Cranberry-Walnut Vinaigrette (recipe below)

Salt and white pepper to taste

12 leaves Belgian endive, trimmed to a V at the bottom

½ cup crumbled Roquefort cheese

¼ cup toasted and coarsely chopped walnuts

¼ cup finely sliced fresh chives

Preheat the oven to 350°F. Lightly oil the beets and place on a cookie sheet. Roast in the oven until tender, 45 minutes to 1 hour, depending on the size of the beets. Cool slightly and peel. Cut into strips ⅛ inch x ⅛ inch x 3 inches. Set aside.

Place the beets, pears, julienned Belgian endive, and shallots in a nonreactive glass bowl. Add the Cranberry-Walnut Vinaigrette. Mix gently but thoroughly to coat well. Add salt and pepper to taste. Place three endive leaves per salad on a chilled plate with the leaves pointing up in a fanlike fashion. Place equal amounts of salad mixture in the center of each plate. Strew the Roquefort and walnuts around the plate and over the salad. Sprinkle chives on top.

CRANBERRY-WALNUT VINAIGRETTE

MAKES 1½ QUARTS

1 tablespoon black peppercorns

1 star anise

½ tablespoon coriander

1 bay leaf

1 sprig thyme

1 whole clove

1 teaspoon juniper berries

4 cups cranberry juice

2 tablespoons peeled and minced shallots

2 teaspoons granulated sugar

½ cup red wine vinegar

Salt and white pepper to taste

2 cups walnut oil

2 cups vegetable oil

Place the black peppercorns, star anise, coriander, bay leaf, thyme, clove, and juniper berries in a small piece of cheesecloth. Fold the cheesecloth and tie with kitchen string, creating an herb sachet.

Add the cranberry juice and herb sachet to a saucepan over medium heat. Continue to cook until volume is reduced by half. Cool and remove the sachet. Add the shallots, sugar, vinegar, salt, and pepper. Slowly whisk in the oils. Chill until ready to use.

TILTH RESTAURANT

1411 NORTH 45TH STREET, SEATTLE
(206) 633-0801
WWW.TILTHRESTAURANT.COM
OWNER: MARIA HINES

As you stroll under the lattice arbor, up the brick-red steps to the green glass door entrance, it may feel as if you're arriving at someone's house for dinner. Welcome to Tilth, the culinary creation of James Beard–Award-winning chef Maria Hines.

Chef Hines's dedication to treating her guests as if they are arriving at her own home has made her restaurant one of the more comfortable and friendly places to dine in Seattle. Whether you come for brunch, prefer something vegan, or choose to taste from one of the popular multicourse dinner tasting menus, Chef Hines will make your dining experience memorable.

Tilth is also one of only two restaurants in the country to receive an Oregon Tilth organic certification, meaning 95 percent of her food is organic. To avoid any quality compromise and to maintain her organic certification, Chef Hines makes many products from scratch, including jam, marmalade, butter, ketchup, mustard, charcuterie, fresh cheeses, pasta, and vinegar. Much of her wine is also organic and pairs well with her wonderful cuisine.

The two featured recipes epitomize Tilth, its commitment to locally grown organic foods and its cooking philosophy. From the farm-fresh cream in the spot prawns, to the use of seasonal root vegetables, both dishes showcase the purest flavor of fresh Northwest ingredients.

Spot Prawns with Baby Chickpeas, Meyer Lemon & Herb Coulis

SERVES 4

Chickpeas:

1 cup dried chickpeas

6 cups cold water, divided

½ medium yellow onion, chopped

1 medium carrot, chopped

2 fresh celery stalks, chopped

2 bay leaves

Salt to taste

Herb Coulis:

1 bunch fresh mint, stems removed

1 bunch fresh cilantro, stems removed

1 bunch fresh Italian parsley, stems removed

3 cloves roasted garlic

Juice of ½ lemon

1 teaspoon kosher salt

½ teaspoon crushed red pepper

3 tablespoons extra-virgin olive oil

Prawns:

4 tablespoons white wine

½ cup heavy cream

1 cup (2 sticks) unsalted butter

1 Meyer lemon (or 1 regular lemon), zested and cut into segments, reserve segments

1 teaspoon kosher salt

1 pinch ground white pepper

1 pound fresh spot prawns, shells removed

1 tablespoon butter

For the chickpeas: Soak the chickpeas overnight in 3 cups of cold water. Drain. Place the chickpeas in a medium-size pot and fill with 3 cups of new water. Add the onions, carrots, celery, and bay leaves. Bring to a simmer for 1 hour, or until tender, but do not boil them. Remove from heat and season with salt. Cool in the liquid.

For the herb coulis: Place the mint, cilantro, parsley, roasted garlic, lemon juice, salt, red pepper, and olive oil in a blender and puree until silky smooth.

For the prawns: Pour the wine into a saucepan over medium heat and reduce until almost evaporated. Add the cream and reduce by half. Cut the butter into small pieces. Over low heat, whisk the butter into the cream, a few pieces at a time. Fully incorporate each batch of butter before adding more, and continue until all the butter has been added. Add lemon zest, salt, and pepper and stir to combine. Add the prawns and cook over low heat until prawns are pink and the tails begin to curl. Remove prawns from the butter.

To serve: In a saucepan over medium heat, melt 1 tablespoon of butter. Add 1 cup of the cooked chickpeas and the reserved lemon segments. Spoon onto serving plates. Top the chickpeas with the cooked prawns. Spoon herb coulis around the plate.

Winter Root Vegetable Salad with Crème Fraîche Vinaigrette

SERVES 4

Root Vegetables:

8 cups cold water

Salt, as needed

¼ cup diced celery root

¼ cup peeled and diced baby carrots

¼ cup diced parsnips

¼ cup diced rutabaga

Beets:

2 large red beets

Olive oil, as needed

Salt and black pepper to taste

2 bay leaves

4 tablespoons kosher salt

2 sprigs fresh thyme

4 cups water

Crème Fraîche Vinaigrette:

1 tablespoon red wine vinegar

1 teaspoon kosher salt

1 pinch white pepper

1 cup crème fraîche

For the root vegetables: In a medium saucepan bring 8 cups of water to a boil. Add enough salt to the water so it tastes like the ocean. Add the celery root and cook until tender, about 4 minutes. Remove celery root from the water and shock in an ice-water bath. Drain. Repeat this step with the carrots, parsnips, and rutabaga.

For the beets: Season the beets heavily with olive oil, salt, and black pepper. In a large casserole or baking dish, combine the beets, bay leaves, salt, thyme, and 4 cups of water. Cover with aluminum foil and bake at 350°F for 45 minutes, or until the beets are knife tender. Remove from oven and cool for 1 hour in the refrigerator. When cool, remove the skins from the beets (using a kitchen towel or gloves will make the process much easier). When peeled, slice the beets paper thin.

For the crème fraîche vinaigrette: In a mixing bowl, combine the vinegar, salt, and pepper. Whisk in the crème fraîche.

To serve: Spiral the beet slices onto serving plates. Use about 6 slices per plate. Mix the root vegetables with the crème fraîche vinaigrette. Place a ring mold in the center of each beet spiral and fill the mold with the root vegetables.

Steel ring molds are available at kitchen stores and online; you can also make one by cutting an empty soup can. (Use caution when preparing the soup can, as some surfaces may be sharp.)

Salty's Seafood Grills

1936 Harbor Avenue Southwest, Seattle
(206) 937-1600
www.saltys.com
Owners: Gerry and Kathy Kingen

This would not be a Seattle cookbook without mentioning Salty's, one of Seattle's iconic waterfront dining establishments. From the moment you enter and see saltwater tanks brimming with live Dungeness crab and Maine lobster, to servers flashing by with large platters of wild sockeye salmon, steamed mussels from local beaches, and bowls of their famous clam chowder, you'll know you've arrived at the right place.

Salty's on Alki Beach is arguably the best establishment in Seattle for Sunday brunch (Salty's also has locations in South Seattle's Redondo Beach and in Portland). In fact, the brunch is so popular they have it on Saturday too. What is better than filling your plate—after plate—with the freshest seafood and your favorite breakfast and lunch items while marveling at incredible panoramic views from across the Sound? Local tip: Get there early, because brunch packs quite a crowd!

Along with Salty's signature brunch, happy hour is a staple for Seattleites. Live music, plenty of draft beers, and fun menu items like an OMG or a Summer Thyme Soda make cocktailing at Salty's a must. If you go, be sure to try the Coconut-Crusted Prawns and the Flaming Lips Clams.

Fennel Pollen Honey-Glazed Salmon Salad

SERVES 2

Fennel Pollen Honey:

¼ cup honey

1 teaspoon fennel pollen or fennel seeds

Salmon:

2 fillets of wild salmon (4–6 ounces each)

Salt and pepper to taste

1 teaspoon canola oil

2 cups arugula

3 tablespoons chèvre cheese

6 raspberries

6 blackberries

6 blueberries

Balsamic Vinaigrette:

2 tablespoons balsamic vinegar

½ teaspoon peeled and minced garlic

1 teaspoon peeled and minced shallot

1 teaspoon minced fresh thyme

½ teaspoon Dijon mustard

⅓ cup olive oil

Salt to taste

To make the fennel pollen honey: Combine the honey and fennel pollen or fennel seeds in a saucepan and simmer over very low heat for 15 minutes. Strain and reserve. (This mixture is also great on fresh bread, toast, or muffins.)

To make the salmon: Season the salmon fillets with salt and pepper, then brush with the fennel pollen honey. In a sauté pan, heat the oil over medium-high heat. Add the salmon and sear on one side for 3 minutes, or until honey caramelizes.

To make the vinaigrette: Mix the vinegar, garlic, shallot, thyme, and Dijon mustard in a mixing bowl. Drizzle in the olive oil and season with salt.

To serve: In a mixing bowl, toss the arugula with the balsamic vinaigrette. Divide the tossed arugula on each serving plate. Place the salmon over the arugula and garnish with the chèvre cheese and fresh berries.

Bastille Café & Bar

5307 Ballard Avenue Northwest, Seattle
(206) 453-5014
www.bastilleseattle.com
Owners: Deming Maclise and James Weimann

It may not appear grand from the outside—an early 1900s brick and window-lined building located on an old street in downtown Ballard—but inside, amid the soft amber lighting, is a treasure trove of architecture and culinary delight. The restaurant byline—"Damn Good French Cuisine"—will remind you of that.

We're talking about Bastille Café & Bar, where owners Deming Maclise and James Weimann scoured Paris flea markets and local salvage stores for vintage accessories to create a truly authentic feel. From the white subway tiles, antique mirrors, and Paris Metro clock, to the zinc-topped bar and stunning crystal chandelier that takes center stage in the back bar, they've truly hit the mark.

Back in the kitchen, Executive Chef Jason Stoneburner, formerly from Colorado, is the culinary artist. He'll top his perfectly roasted pork chop with fresh spring onions from the restaurant's own garden and season his pan-roasted chicken breast just right to bring out the true organic flavors of his sustainable bird. "And don't forget our rabbit pâté with pickled fennel and violet mustard," adds Chef Stoneburner, who finally has been given his own kitchen to command. "We make the mustard too!"

Thanks to a Sunday brunch, happy hour, and late-night dining, you can visit Bastille Café & Bar more than once when craving deliciously fresh Northwest cuisine.

House-Cured Bacon Maison
Warm Cabbage Salad & Chèvre

SERVES 2–4

House-Cured Bacon:

5 pounds pork belly

2½ ounces kosher salt

2 tablespoons brown sugar

¼ teaspoon curing salt

1 tablespoon cracked black pepper, optional

Cabbage Salad:

1 savoy cabbage head

3 tablespoons butter

2 fresh thyme sprigs, leaves picked

2 tablespoons sherry wine vinegar

Salt and pepper to taste

1 cup crumbled fresh goat chèvre

3 tablespoons pine nuts, toasted

To make the house-cured bacon: Rub the pork belly liberally with the salt, sugar, and curing salt. If you would like peppered bacon as an option, add the optional pepper with the salt rub. Wrap the seasoned pork belly in plastic wrap and press between two weighted plates. Refrigerate for 7 days.

Preheat the oven to 325°F. Unwrap the pork belly and place on a baking rack. Bake in the oven until the pork has an internal temperature of 150°F. When the bacon has cooled, remove a small section (about 4 ounces, or ½ cup) and dice it into small cubes. Transfer the cubes to a sauté pan over low heat and slowly cook until crispy. Reserve the rest of the pork in the refrigerator for up to 1 month for another delicious dish.

To make the salad: Remove the core from the cabbage and cut ribbons from the leaves about ½-inch thick. In a large sauté pan over high heat, add the butter and allow to brown slightly. Add about 4 ounces (½ cup) of the house-made bacon, then add the cabbage and sauté lightly until the cabbage turns bright green but remains slightly crunchy. Next, add the thyme and vinegar and adjust with salt and pepper. Remove from the pan to avoid overcooking. Garnish the cabbage with crumbled chèvre and toasted pine nuts. Serve warm.

Arugula & Beet Salad with Pistachio Vinaigrette

SERVES 4 OR 5

Salad:

2 bunches baby beets
Extra-virgin olive oil, as needed
1 bunch fresh arugula
Salt and pepper to taste

Dressing:

4 cups pistachios
¼ cup each chopped fresh thyme, rosemary, and basil
¾ cups extra-virgin olive oil
¼ cup red wine vinegar

Preheat the oven to 325°F. Cut the tops from the beets and wash thoroughly. Place the beets on a cookie sheet and roast in the oven with a small amount of extra-virgin olive oil until tender. Remove from the oven and remove the skins from the beets while they are warm. Quarter the beets.

To make the dressing: Toast and rough chop the pistachios. Combine the chopped thyme, rosemary, and basil with the nuts, olive oil, and vinegar. Toss the beets with the arugula and pistachios. Season with salt and pepper and serve.

The salad pairs well with goat cheese and a glass of Sauvignon Blanc.

HEARTY PASTAS

The first Italian immigrants reached Seattle one hundred years ago. With construction employing workers in large numbers, Italians, along with other immigrants and native-born Americans, shaped much of Seattle as we know it today. Everyone who lived during this time also remembers the redolent smells of Italian cooking that drifted through the neighborhood, especially on Sunday after church. It didn't take long for Seattleites to develop a taste for Italian foods. Today companies such as Oberto and DeLaurenti carry on the tradition, while celebrations like Seattle's Festa Italiana remind everyone that Italian food and wine are here to stay.

Andiamo starts off this chapter with a tasty infusion of Italy and the Pacific Northwest. The result: a spicy spaghetti dish with sweet Dungeness crabmeat. Its penne with sausage, tomato, and porcini is equally divine. Assaggio, where guests are welcomed as if they are visiting the owner's home, also incorporates the Old Country with local flavors, particularly the restaurant's mouthwatering ravioli with wild mushrooms and the rigatoni with locally grown peppers and handcrafted sausage. Seattle's Bizzarro Italian Cafe joins the party with local Manila clams tossed in their popular clam linguine, and the restaurant even takes a moment to teach the home cook how to make fresh gnocchi in the comfort of his or her own kitchen.

Speaking of homemade, La Spiga, the Italian restaurant that's so authentic in both food and ambience you'll feel you've been transported overseas, teaches you step-by-step how to craft tagliatelle and gnocchetti from scratch. Seattle's longtime Italian eateries Il Fornaio and Palomino make guest appearances in the delightful pages ahead with traditional dishes such as penne with a rich tomato-vodka sauce and Sicilian meatballs made with three ground meats—veal, beef, and sausage.

ANDIAMO

938 110th Avenue Northeast, Bellevue
(425) 452-9602
www.andiamobellevue.com
Owner: Reyes Camino

Located in downtown Bellevue, next to the public library, Andiamo Ristorante Italiano is considered one of Eastside's top Italian trattorias.

Take a seat inside and you'll immediately applaud the inviting atmosphere, which is clean, sophisticated, and welcoming. White tablecloths, soft lighting, fresh flowers, and elegant drapes add to the cozy decor. There's also an exhibition-style kitchen, so while sipping your fine Italian Brunello or Chianti you can gawk at the animated cooks, including Alfredo—the executive chef—as they prepare such traditional and authentic dishes as handcrafted Pear and Gorgonzola Ravioli—a house favorite—or the two sumptuous dishes featured here: Penne with Sausage, Tomato & Porcini Sauce, and Spicy Tomato Spaghetti with Fresh Dungeness Crabmeat. "My creativity and attention to detail help me prepare delicious dishes that are as attractive for the palate as for the eyes," says the chef. There is also a vast selection of award-winning wines at Andiamo, with plenty of Italian reds and whites to select from—including half bottles—along with local Washington and California varietals.

Andiamo serves a great lunch, too, and their Grilled Veggie Sandwich or the signature Andiamo Sandwich—spicy coppa, salami, prosciutto, and provolone—are a hit with the neighboring business traffic during the noon hour. *Buon appetito!*

Penne with Sausage, Tomato & Porcini Sauce

SERVES 4

3 teaspoons olive oil, divided

1 teaspoon butter

1 small onion, chopped

½ pound Italian sausage, crumbled into pieces

1 ounce porcini mushrooms

Salt and fresh ground black pepper, to taste

1 (28-ounce) can tomatoes with juice, strained

¼ teaspoon red pepper flakes

12 ounces penne pasta

½ cup heavy cream

2 teaspoons chopped fresh Italian parsley

⅓ cup grated Parmigiana-Reggiano cheese

In a medium sauté pan over low heat, add 1 teaspoon of olive oil and the butter. Add the onions and sauté until soft. Set the onions aside.

In the same pan, heat the remaining oil. Add the sausage and cook until brown. Add the porcini mushrooms to the sausage and cook for 2 minutes. Add the reserved onions and simmer for 10 minutes. Season with salt and pepper. Add the tomatoes and pepper flakes, bring to a boil, and then reduce the heat and simmer for 10 minutes.

Meanwhile, boil the pasta until al dente and set aside. Add the heavy cream to the sauce and heat through.

Before serving, stir the parsley and Parmigiana into the sauce. Add the cooked pasta to the sauce and mix well. Top with extra Parmigiana and serve immediately.

PIKE PLACE MARKET

The Pike Place Market, located in downtown Seattle, is one of the oldest public farmers' markets in the country. Opened in 1907, Pike Place Market is considered one of Seattle's top tourist attractions. Every year more than ten million visitors arrive to buy or just admire the incredibly fresh fruit, produce, meats, seafood, and flowers that adorn the endless food stalls.

One of the more popular attractions is watching the "flying fish" performed by colorful fishmongers. When a whole salmon is purchased, a fishmonger will hurl the three-foot fish across the counter to another monger, who will catch the salmon with his bare hands and quickly fillet or wrap it whole for the customer. It's quite a spectacle for those who've never seen the show.

The market has a variety of offerings, so after admiring the bounty of foods, one can browse stands of unique arts and crafts, admire antique furniture, or take a break from walking and dine at one of the cozy family-owned restaurants nestled inside the market.

Spicy Tomato Spaghetti with Fresh Dungeness Crabmeat

SERVES 4

3 tablespoons butter

1 medium onion, peeled and chopped

1 garlic clove, peeled and crushed

2 red chiles, diced

1 pound fresh garden tomatoes, skinned and diced

¾ cup clam (or seafood) juice

2 tablespoons tomato paste

1 teaspoon sugar

Salt and fresh ground black pepper to taste

1 pound fresh Dungeness crabmeat

12 ounces dried spaghetti

In a large saucepan over medium heat, melt the butter. Add the onion, garlic, and chiles and sauté until soft. Add the tomatoes and juice, reduce heat, and simmer for 10 minutes. Transfer the sauce to a blender and blend until smooth. Return the sauce to the pan, add the tomato paste, sugar, and salt and pepper to taste. Add the crabmeat. Gently reheat and simmer for a couple minutes.

Cook the spaghetti in boiling salted water until al dente. Drain and add the cooked spaghetti to the sauce. Mix well and serve immediately.

Assaggio Ristorante

2010 4th Avenue, Seattle
(206) 441-1399
www.assaggioseattle.com
Owner: Mauro Golmarvi

An old-fashioned building stands along 4th Avenue in downtown Seattle, and two emerald awnings flanked by two colorful, leaved trees funnel you toward the glass door that leads inside Assaggio Ristorante. In addition to being a popular Italian restaurant frequented by some of Seattle's biggest names, *Zagat* rated Assaggio "One of Seattle's Best Restaurants" from 1997 to 2010, and the restaurant received an "Award of Excellence" from 1998 to 2010 from *Wine Spectator.*

Belly up to the bar for a bartender cocktail special like an Aperol Spritz or select an award-winning wine from the extensive list that Assaggio owner Mauro Golmarvi regularly assembles himself. If you happen to be in the bar during happy hour, be sure to order the Meatball Sliders or the deliciously gooey half-priced pizzas.

Dinners at Assaggio are just as authentic as they are in Mauro's homeland, so you can't go wrong with a classic bowl of Tuscan-style white bean soup with prosciutto; any of the house-made pastas, such as the two featured here; or a spin on the classic Caesar salad incorporating fresh wild-caught salmon. Inside tip: To guarantee the freshest ingredients are used, Mauro goes shopping every morning at the famous Seattle Pike Place Market for fresh fish.

As Mauro admits, "It's not about fancy spices or complicated dishes. It's about simplicity, honesty, and passion." Additional signature Italian recipes from Mauro can be found in his cookbook, *Assaggio Ristorante.*

Ravioli Maruzza

RAVIOLI WITH WILD MUSHROOMS

SERVES 4

1 tablespoon unsalted butter

2 cups sliced wild Pacific Northwest mushrooms
    (chanterelles, morels)

¼ cup chopped green onions

Salt and freshly ground black pepper to taste

¼ cup dry red table wine

¼ cup sweet Marsala

¼ cup demi-glace

½ cup heavy cream

½ tablespoon salt

32 large cheese ravioli (premade), available at
    most grocery stores

Combine the butter, mushrooms, green onions,
and salt and pepper to taste in a large sauté pan.
Cook over high heat for 3 to 5 minutes. Add the
red wine, Marsala, demi-glace, and cream, and
continue cooking until the sauce thickens.

Meanwhile, bring 6 quarts of water to a boil
in a large pot and add the ½ tablespoon of
salt. Carefully drop the ravioli into the boiling
water and cook until al dente.

Drain the ravioli and add to the sauce, stirring
to thoroughly coat, and serve.

Rigatoni alla Pepperonata e Salsiccia

Rigatoni with Peppers & Sausage

SERVES 4

2 tablespoons extra-virgin olive oil

4 mild Italian link sausages, sliced

2 red bell peppers, roasted and sliced

1 garlic clove, minced

¼ cup dry red table wine

2 cups marinara (recipe below)

¾ cup heavy cream

6 fresh basil leaves, torn

6 quarts water

½ tablespoon salt

1 pound rigatoni pasta

Freshly shaved Parmesan cheese

Heat the oil in a large saucepan over medium heat. Add the sausage, peppers, and garlic. When sausage is partially cooked, add the wine and continue cooking until reduced, about 6 minutes. Stir in the marinara and cream and cook to reduce by half, and then add the basil.

Meanwhile, bring the water to a boil in a large pot and add the salt. Carefully drop the pasta into the boiling water and cook until al dente.

Drain the pasta and mix with the sauce. Sprinkle with shaved Parmesan and serve.

Marinara

MAKES 6 CUPS

2 tablespoons olive oil

¾ cup chopped onion

2 garlic cloves, chopped

1 cup dry white wine

2 (28-ounce) cans whole peeled plum tomatoes

1 carrot, peeled and quartered lengthwise

1 celery stalk, halved lengthwise

½ teaspoon salt

½ teaspoon freshly ground black pepper

6 fresh basil leaves

Heat the olive oil in a medium sauté pan over medium heat. Add the onion and sauté until translucent. Add the garlic and sauté until it begins to brown.

Add the wine and simmer over medium heat until the alcohol cooks off and the liquid is reduced by half, about 5 minutes. Pour in the tomatoes and mash with a whisk or spoon; bring to a boil.

Bundle the carrots and celery sticks and tie with kitchen string, then add to the sauce. Stir in the salt and pepper, reduce heat to low, and simmer at least 30 minutes, or until the tomatoes break up and the mixture is smooth. Add the basil leaves for the last 10 minutes of cooking. Remove the carrot and celery before using.

Bizzarro Italian Cafe

1307 N. 46th Street, Seattle
(206) 632-7277
WWW.BIZZARROITALIANCAFE.COM
Owners: Jodi-Paul Wooster and Andrew Bray

Featured on the hit show *Diners, Drive-ins and Dives,* Bizzarro Italian Cafe is a culinary gem you should make a point to visit.

With a name like Bizzarro, the restaurant is definitely unique. Located in downtown Wallingford, inside a brick building with multicolor doors and windows, patrons are immediately greeted by bicycles hanging from the ceiling, striking artwork adorning the fire-engine red walls, piano playing, checkered tablecloths, and a lot of comedic restaurant moments. That's because Jodi-Paul Wooster, who co-owns the restaurant with Andrew Bray, comes from an acting, theatrical, and circus background.

The owners (who happen to be former servers at Bizzarro), along with their accomplished chefs, also have a real knack for serving some of the best Italian food around, and that's no laughing matter. Relying on the freshness of locally and organic sourced ingredients, Bizzarro believes in offering high-quality in-season foods. The result is extraordinary dishes like the creamy pumpkin ravioli, the cheesy and meaty lasagna, and the perfectly tender elk shoulder and organic lamb shank.

Without question, the restaurant's most popular dish, featured here, is its signature clam linguine. The dish begins with crispy house-made pancetta that has been soaked in salt for seven days. Added to the pan are hints of garlic, white wine, and roasted jalapeños. Add some local Manila clams and fresh-made linguine, and the end result is an amazing primordial meal for Washingtonians. Enjoy!

CLAM LINGUINE

SERVES 4

4 jalapeños
4 pounds live Manila clams
¼ cup salt
1 cup pancetta
3 tablespoons peeled and crushed garlic
1 cup dry white wine
¼ cup unsalted butter
3 tablespoons chopped fresh flat leaf parsley, divided
1 pound fresh linguine

Start by roasting the jalapeños. Preheat the oven to 350°F. Place the peppers on a baking sheet and roast for 30 minutes, or until tender. Remove from oven and let cool. Remove stems from the peppers, and cut lengthwise. Remove the seeds, then dice the peppers.

In large bowl, rinse the clams under cool tap water with the salt for 5 minutes. Discard any open clams.

Place the pancetta in a large skillet over medium heat and toss until crispy. Stir in the garlic, then add the wine before the garlic browns. Remove from heat and set aside for 2 minutes. Add the clams, return to heat, and cover. When the first clam opens (about 2 to 3 minutes), add the butter and 2 tablespoons of the parsley. Cover and cook until all the clams open (another 2 to 3 minutes). Discard any clams that remain closed.

Carefully drop the fresh linguine in boiling water and cook for 2 minutes. Drain and toss in with clams. Bring the mixture back up to heat and allow sauce to thicken. Top with remaining parsley and serve.

HOUSE-MADE GNOCCHI CAVOLFIORE

SERVES 4

Gnocchi:

5 medium Yukon potatoes

4 large eggs

2 cups flour

Cavolfiore:

1 large garlic bulb

½ cup olive oil

1 medium head cauliflower, cut into small pieces

Salt and pepper to taste

¼ cup water

1 cup heavy cream

½ cup grated Parmesan cheese

To make the gnocchi: Fill a large pot with cold water and add the potatoes. Bring to a gentle boil. Slowly cook the potatoes until tender (when easily pierced with a knife). It is important to use a large volume of water and cook the potatoes as slowly as possible. This "lazy boil" takes approximately 1 hour.

Drain the potatoes and, while still hot, peel them. Transfer the potatoes to a bowl and mash or, preferably, run through a ricer onto a baking sheet and allow for cooling and drying.

Next, crack the eggs into a mixing bowl and mix thoroughly with the potatoes. Add the flour and hand mix. Take a handful of the mixture and rub palm to palm, creating a cohesive softball-size sphere.

Place the ball on a lightly floured surface and roll into a long cylinder just under 1 inch in diameter. Cut 1-inch long gnocchi, then lightly flour to keep ends from sticking. Repeat with the remaining mixture.

Bring a large pot of salted water to a boil. Drop the gnocchi into the water for 2 minutes. Drain in a colander and let cool.

To make the cavolfiore: Preheat the oven to 350°F. Remove the top of the garlic bulb and place in a small oven-safe dish. Pour the olive oil over the top of the bulb. Roast in the oven until soft and caramelized, about 30 minutes. Remove the garlic from the oil; reserve the oil.

In a large skillet, add the reserved oil from the roasted garlic and heat over medium-high heat. Add the cauliflower and sauté until the cauliflower starts to brown. Add salt and pepper to taste. Add ¼ cup of water and remove from heat. Squeeze the garlic bulb, removing the tender meat, and add directly to the skillet. Add the cooked gnocchi, heavy cream, and Parmesan. Mix well to combine. Bring back up to heat, and then serve.

La Spiga

1429 12TH AVENUE, SEATTLE
(206) 323-8881
WWW.LASPIGA.COM
OWNERS: SABRINA TINSLEY AND PIETRO BORGHESI

Perched atop Capitol Hill, Seattle's most populated neighborhood, is Osteria La Spiga. Founded by Sabrina Tinsley and Pietro Borghesi, the casual-yet-classy restaurant with high ceilings, rich woods, exposed architectural accents like the overhead beams, and soft ambient lighting make a great first impression. Spying on the chefs behind glass working in orchestrated chaos in the kitchen is also visually stimulating.

The food at La Spiga is simple—in the tradition of Italy—and very tasty, which is probably why you'll see celebrity chef Mario Batali dropping in from time to time. The pastas—like the potato gnocchi, tagliatelle, and lasagna—are all homemade, as are the accompanying sauces and ragus.

The recipes from La Spiga featured here are two of the owners' favorites that you can create in your own kitchen. "The prosciutto accompanying the tagliatelle comes from hard times in Emilia-Romagna as a way to utilize all parts of the precious prosciutto," Borghesi reveals. "While the gnocchetti is accompanied by a sauce that is more typical of the Umbria region, specifically from the city of Norcia, which is known for its dressed pork products." In fact, *norcino* is the term used to describe pork artisans from this region.

"As a special touch, add truffles in any form to these dishes," adds Tinsley. "Truffles are also typical of dishes from Umbria."

House-Made Tagliatelle al Ragu di Prosciutto

TAGLIATELLE WITH PROSCIUTTO RAGU

SERVES 6

Prosciutto Ragu:

5 fresh garden tomatoes

½ cup (1 stick) butter, divided

1 medium onion, peeled and finely chopped

½ pound prosciutto, thinly sliced

1 cup water

Freshly ground black pepper to taste

1 pat of fresh butter

Parmigiana Reggiano, as needed

Tagliatelle:

5½–6 cups unbleached all-purpose flour

6 large fresh eggs

1 tablespoon olive oil, optional

1 pinch salt

To make the prosciutto ragu: Add water to a small saucepan and bring to a boil. Add the tomatoes and blanch for 2 minutes. Remove tomatoes from the water and shock them in an ice bath. When cool the tomatoes are cool, peel, remove the seeds, and roughly chop.

Place ¼ cup butter in a saucepan over low heat. When melted, add the onion and sauté until tender.

In the meantime, chop the prosciutto until it resembles ground meat, and process the tomatoes in a food processor to a smooth puree. When the onions are tender, add the prosciutto and sauté for about 2 minutes, separating the chunky pieces. Add the tomato puree and the 1 cup water. Bring to a boil, then reduce the heat and simmer for about 20 minutes. The prosciutto should be tender; if not, cook 10 minutes longer. Remove from heat and stir in the remaining ¼ cup butter and season to taste with pepper. Prosciutto is very salty, so additional salt is generally not needed.

To make the tagliatelle: On a work surface (preferably wood) mound 5½ cups of flour and make a well in the center. Drop the eggs, optional olive oil, and salt into the well. With a fork, whisk together the ingredients contained in the well and gradually start pulling in the flour from the borders, equally on all sides; continue this way until the dough becomes stiff enough to work with the hands. Work into a ball and continue to knead until smooth, adding flour as needed to make a stiff dough. Let the dough rest covered with plastic wrap for 30 minutes.

Using a pasta machine, roll out a third of the dough at a time into long thin sheets, and then cut the sheets into shorter pieces approximately 18 inches long. Repeat with the remainder of the dough. Allow the pasta to dry for about 20 minutes, turning the pasta for even drying. When dry, cut the dough on the wider blade of the pasta maker.

To serve: Cook the pasta in boiling water until al dente. Drain and add the pasta to the heated prosciutto ragu. Just before serving, add a pat of fresh butter and plenty of Parmigiana Reggiano. Toss well and serve immediately.

HOUSE-MADE GNOCCHETTI DI RICOTTA E TARTUFO ALLA NORCINA

RICOTTA & TRUFFLE GNOCCHI WITH SAUSAGE & CREAM SAUCE

SERVES 4

Gnocchetti:

2 pounds ricotta cheese

1 egg

Salt and fresh ground black pepper to taste

2 tablespoons truffle flour, optional

2 cups flour, plus extra for dusting

Sauce:

6 Italian sausages

2 tablespoons olive oil

3 tablespoons truffle butter, optional

3 cups heavy cream

Parmigiana Reggiano to taste

Salt to taste

To make the gnocchetti: In a mixing bowl combine the ricotta, egg, salt, a little finely ground black pepper, and the truffle flour, if desired. Add the flour and blend until smooth. The dough should be at a workable consistency and a little sticky. If the dough is too sticky, add a little flour and/or bread crumbs, keeping in mind that too much flour will result in dense and hard gnocchi.

Spread some flour on the surface of the dough, roll the dough into ¼-inch cylinders, cut into ¼-inch pieces, and dust with flour. At this point, if you wish to freeze the gnocchetti for later use, transfer them to freezer bags for convenient storage for up to 3 weeks. If using immediately, transfer gnocchetti to a baking sheet lined with parchment paper. The gnocchetti should be in a single layer.

To make the sauce: Remove the sausages from their casings and sauté in a saucepan over medium heat with the olive oil. When the sausage has just cooked through, add the truffle butter, if desired, and allow to melt before adding the cream. Bring to a boil and remove from heat.

To serve: Boil the gnocchetti (fresh or frozen) in small batches in salted water. In the meantime, heat the sauce. When the gnocchetti float to the surface, strain them and toss them in the sauce, coating thoroughly. Add the Parmigiana Reggiano to taste, season with salt, to taste, and serve immediately.

Il Fornaio

600 Pine Street, Seattle
(206) 264-0994
www.ilfornaio.com
Owner: Il Fornaio (America) Corp.

There doesn't seem to be a shortage of Italian restaurants in Seattle, but for one establishment, the move from Italy to California to the Pacific Northwest has helped differentiate this trattoria from those "other" Italian restaurants.

Founded by Larry B. Mindel, who was impressed by the traditional art of bread making in Milan, Il Fornaio became Mindel's springboard for introducing Americans to the same authentic Italian breads he observed being served throughout Italy. Mindel's Italian bread-baking concept was quickly introduced to the United States thanks to Williams-Sonoma and California, which became the first location in the country to experience such breads. Due to the overwhelming success, Mindel and his Il Fornaio company expanded their culinary menu by adding entrees and opening restaurants throughout California, Las Vegas, and Seattle.

What makes Il Fornaio so special? Some say it's still their crisp rustic bread. Others believe it's the authentic Italian dishes based on real Italian recipes. In Seattle, Chef-Partner Franz Junga makes sure to incorporate high-quality ingredients in his savory menu.

The featured recipes here represent two classic Il Fornaio dishes prepared by Chef Junga: Penne Vodka and Spaghetti alle Cozze. The first dish introduces a creamy and rich mixture of flavors brought out by both the crispy pancetta and tomato-vodka sauce. Spaghetti alle Cozze is a special dish, especially for those in the Pacific Northwest who enjoy their seafood. Chef Junga takes the time to select the freshest and best mussels available, which stand out in this exceptional dish.

PENNE VODKA

RIBBED PASTA TUBES IN A CREAMY TOMATO-VODKA SAUCE

SERVES 6

3 tablespoons olive oil, divided

9 ounces pancetta, sliced ¼-inch thick, unrolled into strips, and julienned

2 shallots, minced

1 cup vodka

1½ cups heavy whipping cream

1 cup Salsa di Pomodoro (recipe at right)

5 quarts (20 cups) water

5 teaspoons sea salt

1 pound dry penne rigate

¹/₃ cup freshly grated Parmigiana Reggiano

1 tablespoon chopped fresh Italian parsley

Heat 2 tablespoons of the olive oil in a large nonstick sauté pan over medium-high heat. Add the pancetta and cook until crispy, about 5 minutes. Drain the excess fat from the pan by tilting the pan and spooning out the oil collected on the side.

Add the remaining 1 tablespoon of olive oil to the sauté pan and heat over medium-high heat. Add the shallots and cook until soft, about 3 minutes. Add the vodka. Bring to a boil and cook until reduced by half, 6 to 7 minutes. Add the cream and cook until reduced by half, about 5 minutes. Add the Salsa di Pomodoro and bring to a boil. Reduce the heat to low and keep warm while the pasta is cooking.

Bring the water and sea salt to a boil in a large stockpot over high heat. Add the penne and cook until al dente. Transfer to a colander to drain. Add the pasta to the pan with the Salsa di Pomodoro and toss to coat evenly. Transfer to a serving platter and sprinkle with Parmigiana and parsley.

SALSA DI POMODORO

MAKES APPROXIMATELY 2 CUPS

2 pounds ripe tomatoes or 1 (28-ounce) can whole peeled tomatoes with juice

3 tablespoons olive oil

¹/₃ medium yellow onion, peeled and diced

2 garlic cloves, smashed

½ dried pepperocini, broken into small pieces

6 fresh medium basil leaves, torn into small pieces

2 tablespoons chopped fresh oregano

¼ teaspoon sea salt

¼ teaspoon fresh ground pepper

If you are using fresh tomatoes, bring 4 quarts of water to a boil in a large stockpot. Cut a small X in the bottom of each tomato. Drop the tomatoes into the boiling water and remove after 15 to 20 seconds. Let cool slightly, peel, and cut out the core. Cut each tomato in half and, using your thumb, scoop out the seeds. Cut each tomato into quarters and set aside. If you are using canned tomatoes, pour the tomatoes with their juice into a large bowl and break the tomatoes into smaller pieces with your hands; set aside.

Heat the olive oil in a medium saucepan over medium-high heat. Add the onion, garlic, and pepperocini. Cook until the onion is tender, 3 to 5 minutes. Add the tomatoes, basil, oregano, salt, and pepper. Bring to a boil, reduce heat to a simmer, and cook, uncovered, 30 minutes. Transfer mixture to a food mill and puree over a bowl. Use immediately or store, refrigerated, in an airtight container.

Spaghetti alle Cozze

MUSSELS, ANCHOVIES & TOMATOES
TOSSED WITH PASTA STRANDS

SERVES 6

Mussels:

¼ cup olive oil

2¾ pounds mussels, well rinsed and de-bearded

4 garlic cloves, smashed

1 tablespoon chopped fresh Italian parsley

Freshly ground pepper

½ lemon

½ cup dry white wine

Tomato Sauce:

⅓ cup olive oil

5 anchovy fillets, chopped

4 garlic cloves, smashed

1 dried pepperocini, broken into small pieces

1 (28-ounce) can plus 1 cup whole peeled tomatoes,
   with their juice, sliced into thin strips

½ cup firmly packed fresh basil leaves,
   torn into small pieces

Spaghetti:

5 quarts (20 cups) water

5 teaspoons sea salt

1 pound spaghetti

2 tablespoons extra-virgin olive oil

2 tablespoons chopped fresh Italian parsley

To prepare the mussels: Heat the olive oil in a large, high-sided sauté pan over high heat. Add the mussels, garlic, parsley, and a pinch of pepper. Quickly squeeze the lemon over the mussels, then add it to the pan. Add the wine and cover. Cook until the mussels begin to open, 1 to 2 minutes. Be careful not to overcook.

Spread the mussels on a baking sheet to cool. Once cool, remove the mussels from their shells by gently scrapping with a small spoon. Discard the shells. Strain the liquid from the sauté pan into a medium saucepan and bring to a boil over medium-high heat. Cook until reduced by half, 2 to 3 minutes.

To prepare the tomato sauce: Heat the olive oil in a large sauté pan over medium-high heat. Add the anchovies, garlic, and pepperocini; cook 1 minute. Add the tomatoes and basil; cook 15 minutes. Add the reduced liquid from the mussels. Bring to a boil and continue to boil until the sauce becomes thick, 35 to 40 minutes.

To prepare the spaghetti: Bring the water and sea salt to a boil in a large stockpot over high heat. Add the spaghetti and cook until al dente. Transfer to a colander to drain. Add the spaghetti to the pan with the tomato sauce and toss to coat evenly. Add the mussels, extra-virgin olive oil, and parsley. Toss to mix well.

PALOMINO RESTAURANT & BAR

1420 FIFTH AVENUE, SEATTLE
(206) 623-1300
WWW.PALOMINO.COM
OWNER: RESTAURANTS UNLIMITED INC.

Palomino Restaurant & Bar is the perfect place for an exceptional cocktail or delicious meal before catching a movie, doing some shopping, or simply loosening the tie after work. It's also the perfect spot to meet for lunch. Despite being recognized as a national chain, Palomino is classy, sophisticated, and very popular with both Seattle and Bellevue residents.

Happy hour is always a surefire hit at Palomino and can draw quite the crowd. That's because many like to migrate to the bar for a fresh-made Pomegranate Margarita, Cranberry Mojito, or White Wine Sangria while snacking on delicious brick oven-fired pizza specials. The bruschetta is also highly sought after because of the many variations it offers besides the common tomato basil, such as Eggplant Caponato and Roasted Pepper–Capacollo.

The recipes by Palomino featured here are Truffle Pea Trenne and Sicilian Meatballs. The Truffle Pea Trenne is a delicious, robust dish made with a rich combination of cream, Parmigiana Reggiano, spring peas, crisp prosciutto, and truffle oil. It's a simple and savory dish for friends and family. The meatballs are served in a rich marinara sauce and are always spicy and full flavored. They are perfect on their own or served on a soft potato roll, as they are for the restaurant's popular Meatball Sliders.

Truffle Pea Trenne

SERVES 2

2 thin slices prosciutto

1 teaspoon olive oil

8 ounces trenne (or penne) pasta

2 tablespoons olive oil

1 tablespoon minced shallot

1 teaspoon minced garlic

6 ounces mixed fresh peas (shucked English peas, julienned snap peas, and/or snow peas)

2 ounces prosciutto, cut into julienne strips

1 teaspoon finely chopped fresh flat-leaf parsley

½ teaspoon finely chopped fresh basil

½ teaspoon finely chopped fresh oregano

¼ teaspoon finely chopped fresh thyme

1½ cups whipping cream

2 tablespoons freshly grated Parmigiana Reggiano, plus some thinly shaved for serving

½ teaspoon white truffle oil

Sea salt and freshly ground black pepper, to taste

Begin by making prosciutto crisps: Preheat the oven to 300°F. Line a rimmed baking sheet with a silicone baking mat or parchment paper. Lightly brush both sides of the prosciutto slices with olive oil and lay them in a single layer on the prepared baking sheet. Bake until crisp, 15 to 20 minutes. Set aside to cool. When cool, break into large, rustic pieces.

Bring a large saucepan of salted water to a boil. Add the pasta and boil until al dente, 10 to 12 minutes.

While the pasta is cooking, heat the olive oil in a medium skillet over medium heat. Add the shallot and garlic and cook, stirring, until tender and aromatic, 1 to 2 minutes. Add the peas and cook until just brightened in color and partly tender,

1 to 2 minutes. Stir in the julienned prosciutto, parsley, basil, oregano, and thyme, then add the cream. Simmer until the cream is reduced by about half, 3 to 5 minutes.

When the pasta is ready, drain well and add to the pea sauce with the grated cheese and truffle oil. Toss gently to mix, then taste for seasoning, adding salt and pepper if necessary.

To serve: Spoon the pasta into individual shallow bowls and top with prosciutto crisps. Scatter shaved Parmigiana Reggiano over the top and serve immediately.

DELAURENTI SPECIALTY FOOD & WINE

Anyone who enjoys cooking Italian food in Seattle is familiar with DeLaurenti. This historic Italian specialty food and wine shop located at the Pike Place Market is filled with authentic ingredients from the Old Country—a testament to the shop's ongoing commitment to providing home cooks with the smells and tastes of Italy. From the wide assortment of artisan breads, cheeses, meats, wines, and a tempting selection of chocolates, to walls of olive oil, canned tomatoes, and every pasta shape imaginable, DeLaurenti is a must-stop shopping destination for preparing Italian dinners in Seattle.

SICILIAN MEATBALLS

SERVES 4–6

Tomato Sauce:

¼ cup extra-virgin olive oil

½ onion, peeled and cut into ¼-inch dice

2 tablespoons minced garlic

2 tablespoons chopped fresh basil

2 (28-ounce) cans whole pear tomatoes in juice
(such as San Marzano), crushed by hand

Salt and pepper to taste

Meatballs:

3 tablespoons olive oil, divided

2 tablespoons minced onion

1 teaspoon minced garlic

1 egg

1/3 cup panko bread crumbs

1 tablespoon grated Pecorino Romano cheese

1 tablespoon minced fresh basil

1 tablespoon minced fresh Italian parsley

¼ teaspoon crushed red pepper

¼ teaspoon black pepper

½ pound ground veal

½ pound ground beef

½ pound ground hot Italian sausage

¼ teaspoon kosher salt

Garnish:

Citrus cheese:

    3 tablespoons grated Pecorino Romano cheese

    ½ teaspoon lemon zest

    ½ teaspoon lime zest

    ½ teaspoon orange zest, all finely minced

    1 teaspoon chopped fresh Italian parsley

2 teaspoons toasted and coarsely chopped pistachios

Pinch crushed red pepper

To make the tomato sauce: Heat the oil in a 2-quart saucepan. Add the onions and garlic and sweat until onions are translucent. Add the basil, tomatoes with juice, and season to taste with salt and pepper. Let simmer for 30 to 45 minutes, or until sauce just coats the back of a spoon.

To make the meatballs: Heat half of the olive oil in a sauté pan over medium-high heat. Add the onions and garlic and sweat until translucent. Remove the onion-garlic mixture from the pan and transfer to a mixing bowl. Add the egg, bread crumbs, cheese, basil, parsley, crushed red pepper, and black pepper. Mix well to incorporate. Add the ground meats and salt. Mix well, then form mixture into 1-ounce (golf ball–size) meatballs.

Heat the remaining olive oil in the sauté pan. Add the meatballs and brown on all sides. Add the hot tomato sauce and allow to cook for 15 minutes.

Place the citrus cheese ingredients in a small bowl and toss well to combine. Remove the meatballs and sauce from the heat and top with citrus cheese, pistachios, and crushed red pepper. Serve warm.

Fish & Shellfish

Seattle's proximity to the Pacific Ocean, from Oregon to Alaska, ensures that the finest fish and shellfish are delivered right to its docks every day. Whether one is buying a freshly caught salmon right off a boat in Ballard's Fishermen's Terminal, or having a live Dungeness crab plucked from a tank at the world-famous Pike Place Market, Seattle is synonymous with an abundance of delicious high-quality seafood. For restaurateurs in the area, there's no shortage of seafood ideas to put on the menu.

In this chapter, Mexico-inspired Barrio selects fresh Northwest seafood in its Rockfish & Grilled Prawn Ceviche, while Bellevue's Bis on Main creates two exciting dishes with local fish—one salt water, one freshwater—in its curried halibut cheeks and bacon-wrapped rainbow trout. Cafe Juanita and James Beard Award–winner Holly Smith unveil her coveted Alaska spot prawns in her two signature dishes: Spot Prawns with Citrus Risotto and Spot Prawn Brodetto. Elliott's Oyster House incorporates two Northwest seafood staples in its Alder Planked King Salmon with Smoked Tomato Beurre Blanc and Spicy Grilled Dungeness Crab dishes.

Not to be outdone, James Beard Award–winner Christine Keff and her Flying Fish Restaurant step up with two sumptuous recipes of her own featuring another Northwest favorite—lingcod. Her marinated lingcod and lingcod tacos please both Seattle residents and visitors alike. Rover's takes a quick departure on the Northwest theme by featuring Mediterranean and Japanese flavors, such as mackerel with tomato confit and caper vinaigrette and tuna sashimi, while Trellis and Aqua by El Gaucho (formerly Waterfront Seafood Grill) return to the Northwest's watery backyard. Trellis shares its savory Alaskan halibut and pan-seared wild salmon recipes, and Aqua teases the taste buds with stuffed prawns and a rich and creamy Dungeness crab mac and cheese.

Barrio Mexican Kitchen & Bar

1420 12th Avenue, Seattle
(206) 588-8105
WWW.BARRIORESTAURANT.COM
Owners: Larry and Tabitha Kurosky

If you're looking for a fun, urban, energetic scene coupled with fantastic Mexican food, visit Barrio Mexican Kitchen & Bar. Located in Seattle's vibrant Capital Hill, between Pike and Union, Barrio is the Pacific Northwest's version of "South of the Border." With more than three hundred candles lit by hand, a massive bar, and stylish decor including industrial elements like massive roll-up windows and solid wood doors with wrought-iron hinges, patrons come here to have a really good time, just as if they're vacationing in Mexico. Whether you come in for drinks or stay for dinner, Barrio promises you will leave satisfied.

The specialty cocktails, from the House Margarita to the Burninator, are made with care by some of the best mixologists in town. Seattle owners Larry and Tabitha Kurosky, who also own Purple Café & Wine Bar, know a thing or two about the importance of serving quality libations—Larry used to work the bar when the couple opened their first Purple restaurant in 2001.

The Barrio food is equally intoxicating. Using a modern approach to Mexican-inspired cuisine, the restaurant features many distinct dishes such as fresh guacamole made to order, Wagyu beef sliders, and pork belly braised with—yes, not a misprint—Coca-Cola.

Highlighted here is a very Mexican dish from Barrio using two fresh Northwest ingredients. The Rockfish & Grilled Prawn Ceviche illustrates the flavors and textures of locally caught fish and shellfish, and the seafood pairs extremely well with the mango, onion, chile peppers, cucumber, and fresh cilantro.

ROCKFISH & GRILLED PRAWN CEVICHE

SERVES 6-8

2 pounds fresh Northwest rockfish fillets

2 cups fresh lime juice

1 pound fresh cold-water prawns

2 tablespoons salt, divided

½ cup diced ripe mango

¼ cup diced red onion

2 tablespoons diced Serrano chile

2 tablespoons diced Fresno chile

½ cup diced cucumber, peeled and deseeded

¼ bunch fresh cilantro, minced

2 limes

1 orange

Yucca chips or corn chips, as needed

Cut the rockfish into small pieces and transfer to a glass bowl. Cover the fish with the lime juice and let it "cook" in the refrigerator for 3 hours.

Peel and devein the prawns. Toss the prawns with 1 tablespoon salt and cook on a hot grill or outdoor barbecue, about 2 minutes on each side. Cool the shrimp and cut into small pieces.

After the rockfish has "cooked" in the lime juice, drain the juice, leaving only the fish. Add the grilled prawns to the bowl, along with the mango, onion, chile peppers, cucumber, cilantro, and remaining 1 tablespoon of salt. Slice the limes and orange in half and squeeze the juices over the fish mixture. Toss everything until well combined and add more salt as needed.

Serve with yucca chips or corn chips.

BIS ON MAIN

10213 MAIN STREET, BELLEVUE
(425) 455-2033
WWW.BISONMAIN.COM
OWNER: JOE VILARDI

Bis on Main offers the best in contemporary Northwest cuisine from one of the hottest restaurants on the Seattle Eastside. The restaurant's popular menu features signature cocktails, dazzling appetizers and small plates, crisp salads, creamy soups, hearty sandwiches, fresh seafood, traditional pastas and risottos, prime meats and poultry, and sinfully delicious desserts.

Owner Joe Vilardi, who entered the restaurant industry as a pot scrubber at age fourteen and worked his way up the ladder, from catering gigs in Detroit and culinary experiences in France, to working the room at the famed The Palm Restaurant and Spago in Beverly Hills, has a straightforward motto: Make Bis on Main the very best it can be by offering quality, service, and honesty.

With its intimate dining room filled with beautiful art and perfect lighting, guests at Bis always know what to expect, especially when it comes to the food. The restaurant attracts a long list of regulars, many of whom are high-profile locals, and Joe and his culinary team make sure to make them feel at home while delivering consistency day in and day out. New chef Remi Dubois does his part in the kitchen by creating sensational selections including the coveted crispy garlic chicken and the always fresh seafood like the two featured recipes: curried halibut cheeks and bacon-wrapped rainbow trout from Alaska's icy waters.

CURRIED HALIBUT CHEEKS WITH BEETS, GRAPEFRUIT & DILL EMULSION

SERVES 4–6

½ pound red beets

½ pound golden beets

1 cup extra-virgin olive oil

1½ tablespoons kosher salt, divided

1½ teaspoons black pepper, divided

1 pound rock salt

2 ruby red grapefruit

¼ cup rice wine vinegar

½ teaspoon Dijon mustard

2 tablespoons finely minced shallot

2 tablespoons finely chopped baby dill

2 pounds fresh halibut cheeks

¼ cup yellow curry powder

Dill sprigs for garnish

Preheat the oven to 425°F.

Toss the beets with 2 tablespoons olive oil, ½ tablespoon salt, and ½ teaspoon black pepper. Place the rock salt on a baking sheet, loosely wrap each beet in foil, and place them on the rock salt and into the oven. Roast until just tender; depending on the size, this could take about 45 minutes. Check the beets by piercing them with a bamboo skewer. If the skewer sinks in with a slight amount of resistance, they are done. Remove the beets and cool before peeling. Once the beets are cool, use a kitchen towel or paper towel (rubber gloves work well too) and rub the skins off. Be sure to peel the golden beets first, because the red beets will bleed over everything. Once the golden beets are peeled, use a vegetable slicer or mandolin to slice them thin (if the beets are too large, cut them in half). Set them aside and repeat with the red beets.

Remove the ends from the grapefruit and remove the rind down to the flesh. Section the grapefruit and collect the juice. Reserve the sections and strain the juice into a small saucepan. Over medium heat, reduce the juice by half and then allow to cool.

In a mixing bowl, whisk together the juice, rice wine vinegar, ½ teaspoon salt, ½ teaspoon black pepper, and mustard. While whisking, add ⅔ cup of the oil in a slow steady stream. Stir in the shallots, grapefruit sections, chopped dill, and check the seasoning. Refrigerate until ready to use.

Season the halibut cheeks on both sides with salt and pepper and dredge one side with yellow curry powder. In a large sauté pan over medium-high heat, add the remaining olive oil. When hot, lay the cheeks in, curry side up. Sauté until light brown, about 2 minutes. Turn over and sauté until a deep yellow-brown color develops, about 4 minutes. Remove and set aside.

To serve, arrange the chilled beets in an overlapping spiral pattern on individual plates, being sure to alternate the golden and red beets. Season the beets with salt and pepper. Ladle some of the grapefruit juice mixture onto and around the beets. Make sure the grapefruit pieces are in some sort of pattern. Lay the halibut cheeks in a shingled pattern across the middle of the plate, over the beets, at least 3 pieces per person. Garnish with dill sprigs.

Bacon-Wrapped Trout with Lentils, Currants & Hazelnuts

SERVES 4–6

5 tablespoons olive oil

½ small yellow onion, peeled and small diced

1 tablespoon minced garlic

3 cups French green lentils

2 quarts chicken stock

¼ cup hazelnuts, toasted and roughly chopped

¼ cup dried black currants

2 teaspoons fresh rosemary, finely chopped

2½ tablespoons salt

1 tablespoon black pepper

4 whole Idaho rainbow trout, head and tail on, backbone, pin bones and fins removed

1 lemon

8 strips thinly cut bacon

½ cup unsalted butter

½ cup white wine

1½ tablespoons chopped fresh thyme

Preheat the oven to 450°F.

To make the lentils: In a sauce pot over high heat, add 1 tablespoon olive oil. When the oil is hot, add the onion and garlic, stirring frequently until lightly brown, about 5 minutes. Add the lentils and chicken stock, bring to a simmer, then reduce heat to medium-low. Cook until the lentils are just done (not too soft), about 20 minutes. Drain the lentils if there is excess liquid.

Place the lentils back in the pan, toss in the hazelnuts, currants, rosemary, 1 tablespoon salt, ½ teaspoon pepper, and toss well to combine. Keep warm.

To make the trout: Open the trout and sprinkle a little salt and pepper inside. Cut the lemon in half and squeeze a little juice (no seeds) on the inside of each fish. Close the trout, pat the outsides dry

with paper towels, and use the remaining salt and pepper to season the outside of the four fish. Now lay 2 strips of bacon, touching side by side, on a cutting board. Square off the ends by cutting off about ¼ inch. The bacon strips should be long enough to overlap by about an inch once they're wrapped around the fish. Lay one of the trout across the center of the bacon and wrap with bacon. Transfer to a platter and repeat the process with the remaining fish.

In a large cast iron skillet or sauté pan over medium-high heat, add 2 tablespoons olive oil. Swirl the oil around to coat the pan, and, when hot, gently lay the trout down and sear (2 trout per pan if possible). Cook until the bacon begins to tighten and crisp, about 5 minutes. With a fish spatula, gently flip the fish over, add 1 tablespoon butter, and cook until the bacon crisps, about 3 minutes. Transfer the fish to an oiled baking sheet and repeat the process for the other fish. Place the baking sheet with the 4 fish in the oven for another 5 minutes.

While the fish is finishing, pour the excess oil out of the pan, turn the heat to high and add the wine. Using the back of a spatula, scrape up any of the flavorful bits and reduce the wine by half. Add the chopped thyme, a little salt and pepper, and swirl in the remaining butter. Turn the heat off.

To serve: Spoon an oblong-shaped portion of the lentils onto each of four dinner platters. Lay a trout on the lentils, and spoon some of the pan sauce on and around the fish. Serve with a side vegetable such as creamed corn.

CAFE JUANITA

9702 NORTHEAST 120TH PLACE, KIRKLAND
(425) 823-1505
WWW.CAFEJUANITA.COM
OWNER: HOLLY SMITH

Tucked on a side street in Juanita—a quaint little neighborhood along the northeast shore of Lake Washington—beneath a canopy of trees, sits a very unassuming restaurant. Step inside and you've suddenly been transported to the lovely and peaceful lake shores of Northern Italy.

The atmosphere of Cafe Juanita—one of the premier and upscale restaurants on the Eastside—is warm and inviting, and the open kitchen creates an intimate environment to make you feel as if you are at home with someone cooking for you. The staff—from wine stewards to servers—make Cafe Juanita one of the best when it comes to impeccable service. The food is equally exceptional, which is why Cafe Juanita continues to rank as one of the top restaurants in the state. Cafe Juanita is also known for teaming up with local farms and purveyors to acquire the best organic and sustainable ingredients available.

Led by culinary maestro and James Beard Award–winning chef Holly Smith, Cafe Juanita specializes in creative Italian cuisine, and it's clear in her approach that Chef Smith cares about what she's making and serving. Paired with some of the most sought-after wines from the Northwest, unique, succulent—and often gluten-free—dishes include Fried Rabbit Liver, Bone Marrow Bruschetta, Smoked Sablefish, and Grilled Octopus. No other restaurant competes when it comes to uniqueness. Just make sure to arrive a little early, because parking can be difficult.

LAKE WASHINGTON

Lake Washington is a large, beautiful freshwater lake that separates Seattle from neighboring Eastside; two concrete floating bridges span the lake north and south. Carved by glaciers thousands of years ago, Lake Washington is the place for summer recreation, including waterskiing, Jet-Skiing and pleasure boating, fishing, canoeing, and sightseeing. Many prominent Seattle residents live on the shorelines of Lake Washington, including Microsoft billionaires Steve Ballmer and co-founders Paul Allen and Bill Gates. During the first week in August, boaters and partygoers flock to the lake for the annual Seafair festival, which dates back to 1950. Events include ship tours, parades, and street performances, but the two main attractions that draw tens of thousands of visitors—rain or shine—are the hydroplane races and the aerial stunts of the Navy's Blue Angels.

Spot Prawns with Citrus Risotto

SERVES 4–6

Citrus:

2 blood oranges

1 navel orange

1 Meyer (or regular) lemon

1 lime

Prawns:

¾ pound Alaska spot prawns, cleaned and
shells removed

2 tablespoons chopped chives

1 tablespoon chopped flat-leaf parsley

Kosher salt to taste

Risotto:

1 medium yellow onion

3 ounces Pecorino cheese

6 cups chicken stock (fish stock or vegetable
stock may be substituted)

3 tablespoons plus 1 stick unsalted butter

1¼ cups raw carnaroli rice (Italian short-grain rice)

¼ cup dry white wine

Pumpkin seed oil or balsamic vinegar, for garnish

To prepare the citrus: Using a sharp paring knife,
cut off both ends of the blood oranges, navel
orange, lemon, and lime. Do this over a bowl to
capture their juice. Remove the peels and piths to
expose only the citrus. Following the membrane
with the knife, remove the individual segments of
the fruit and set aside. Reserve the juice for later.

To prepare the prawns: In a small bowl, combine
the prawns, chives, and flat-leaf parsley. Season
lightly with kosher salt and toss. Set aside.

To prepare the risotto: Peel and dice the onion.
Grate the Pecorino. In a heavy saucepan,
bring the stock to a simmer. In separate heavy
saucepan on medium heat, add 3 tablespoons
butter. Add the onions and sauté 3 to 5 minutes,
until soft and slightly golden. Add the rice and
stir with a wooden spoon to coat. Deglaze with
the white wine and the reserved citrus juice.
Then add the stock, 1 cup at a time, to the rice
mixture. The rice will slowly absorb the liquid.
After 3 cups stock have been added, taste the
rice for doneness. It should be moist, creamy,
and just tender. If necessary, add more liquid
and cook longer. When the rice is done, remove
from the heat. Beat in the stick of butter, working
quickly until it is well incorporated. Add the grated
Pecorino cheese and season with kosher salt.
Return the pan to the heat to ensure the cheese
is well incorporated.

Add the seasoned spot prawns to the rice. Turn
off the heat and gently fold in to cook the prawns,
about 1 to 2 minutes.

To serve: Divide the prawn risotto mixture among
individual serving plates and top with a drizzle of
pumpkin seed oil or balsamic vinegar.

Spot Prawn Brodetto

SERVES 4–6

1½ cups satsuma juice (any fresh mandarin orange, tangerine, or clementine works well)

Pinch of salt

Dash of lemon or lime juice, optional

1 medium Yukon gold potato, diced small

6–8 tablespoons unsalted butter, divided

½ fennel bulb, diced small

1 large shallot, finely minced

1 clove garlic, finely minced

Pinch of kosher salt to taste

2 ounces white wine

3 cups crème fraîche

Cayenne pepper to taste

1 lemon, half zest and half juice

2 pounds Alaska spot prawns, shells removed, roe separated and reserved, and meat roughly chopped

Fresh cracked black pepper

3 tablespoons finely chopped chives, for garnish

Begin by making a satsuma reduction: Combine the satsuma juice with the salt in a saucepan and cook over medium heat. Allow the juice to slowly reduce to a thin consistency. The sauce will thicken further as it cools. Season with salt, and if the sauce is too sweet (depends on the fruit), add a dash of lemon or lime juice to accentuate the acidity.

Blanch the Yukon potatoes in boiling salted water. When they're just tender, remove from heat and shock the potatoes in an ice bath to stop the cooking process.

In a medium heavy-bottomed pot, heat 4 tablespoons butter until melted. Add in the fennel bulb and sauté until just tender. Keep the pot on the heat and move the fennel bulb off to one side.

Add 1 tablespoon butter, if necessary, and add the minced shallot and garlic. Sauté evenly. You want to sauté all the shallots and garlic separate from the fennel bulb to ensure the shallots and garlic are well sweated with no raw garlic flavor, so don't skimp on the butter. When the shallots and garlic are just beginning to turn golden, stir together with the fennel bulb and add the potatoes. Season lightly with kosher salt and deglaze the pot with white wine.

Add the crème fraîche and a tiny pinch of cayenne and bring to a simmer. Taste and adjust the salt. Next, add the lemon zest and, if necessary, some lemon juice. (Note: Your crème fraiche will vary in acidity, so adjust for flavor.) Whisk in 2 tablespoons butter.

Next, prepare the raw spot prawn meat by seasoning it with kosher salt and a little cracked black pepper. Turn off the heat on the soup and stir in the prawn meat. (Note: The prawn meat will be cooked by the heat of the soup and remain very tender and sweet.)

At the last moment, stir in the prawn roe. (Note: The roe will need to be removed from the prawns and worked through your fingers to separate. If this step isn't done, there will be strings and clumps of roe.)

Divide mixture among individual serving dishes and top with a light drizzle of the satsuma reduction. Garnish with chives and serve immediately.

Elliott's Oyster House

1201 Alaskan Way, Seattle
(206) 623-4340
www.elliottsoysterhouse.com
Owner: Consolidated Restaurants Inc.

From the shade-grown coffee to the wild-caught salmon, Elliott's Oyster House, one of Seattle's most beloved seafood restaurants, believes in protecting our fragile environment through sustainability and being proactive.

Situated on Pier 56, inside a large green building that resembles an oversize boat shed, Elliott's is a friendly gathering place for those seeking responsibly sourced food, a cozy bar, and fresh shucked oysters that are ridiculously inexpensive during happy hour. In fact, during the week Elliott's will shuck more than 7,000 oysters.

But it's not just the oysters that have people waiting in line for a table.

Obviously Seattle is synonymous with salmon. And at Elliott's the plank salmon is a fan favorite. Executive Chef Robert Spaulding's Alder Planked King Salmon with Smoked Tomato Beurre Blanc features a signature spice mixture that complements the rich flavor and texture of the fish and forms a crust as it cooks. "The Smoked Tomato Beurre Blanc adds to the complexity of flavor," he says. "We suggest an alder plank for mild flavor that does not overwhelm the salmon."

Chef Spaulding is especially known for his Spicy Grilled Dungeness Crab, which is featured here. "The Thai sweet chile flavors of the spicy crab sauce accentuate the sweetness of the crab without overpowering its flavor," he reveals. "If possible, prepare the dish on the grill, as the caramelization of the sauce from the direct heat is wonderful."

ALDER PLANKED KING SALMON WITH SMOKED TOMATO BEURRE BLANC

SERVES 4

Salmon Rub (makes approximately 1 pound):

¾ pound brown sugar

1 teaspoon chili powder

1 tablespoon dry thyme

10 tablespoons kosher salt

1 tablespoon course black pepper

½ cup paprika

¼ teaspoon cayenne pepper

2 tablespoons chopped fresh thyme

¼ teaspoon ground white pepper

Smoked Tomato Beurre Blanc (makes approximately 1 cup):

4 Roma tomatoes, cut into ¼-inch dice

½ red onion, cut into ¼-inch dice

½ teaspoon kosher salt, divided

1/8 teaspoon freshly cracked black pepper

2 cups alder chips

2 teaspoons minced shallots

1 tablespoon fresh lemon juice

3 tablespoons white wine

1½ teaspoons heavy cream

½ pound unsalted butter, cut into 1-inch cubes

Salmon:

1 (7x13) alder plank

¼ cup olive oil, divided

4 fillets fresh king salmon, 6–8 ounces each

To make the salmon rub: In a mixing bowl, combine the brown sugar, chili powder, dry thyme, salt, black pepper, paprika, cayenne pepper, chopped thyme, and white pepper; toss until evenly mixed. Store in a clean container until needed.

To make the smoked tomato beurre blanc: Toss the diced tomatoes, onion, ¼ teaspoon salt, and pepper in a mixing bowl. Spread tomato mixture on a baking sheet.

Soak 2 cups alder chips in water for 20 minutes, then drain and place on a sheet of aluminum foil. Place the foil over the heating element of a gas or charcoal grill. Turn on the grill and heat until the chips begin to smoke and glow. Turn off the grill and place the baking sheet with the tomato mixture on it over the top of the alder chips; cover the grill. Let the tomatoes smoke for 20 minutes, then remove and chill.

Combine the shallots, lemon juice, and wine in a small saucepan and reduce by half over medium heat; strain, reserving the liquid. Return the strained liquid to the saucepan and add the cream. Cook for 1 minute. Working on and off the heat, whisk in the butter, one piece at a time, to form an emulsion. Stir in ¼ teaspoon salt and the smoked tomatoes and keep warm.

To make the salmon: Preheat the oven to 450°F. Rub both sides of an alder plank with olive oil. Preheat the plank in the oven for 15 minutes, then remove plank from oven. Brush both sides of the salmon fillets with olive oil and then coat evenly with the salmon rub. Place fillets skin side down on the plank. Place planked salmon in the preheated oven and roast for 5 minutes. Remove from oven and turn salmon over. Return to oven and roast approximately 6 to 7 minutes, or just until salmon loses its translucency. Remove to a warm serving platter (or serve on the plank or individual warm plates) and ladle ⅛ cup smoked tomato beurre blanc diagonally across the fillets.

SPICY GRILLED DUNGENESS CRAB

SERVES 4

1½ cups Thai sweet chili sauce

1½ cups olive oil

2½ tablespoons chopped garlic

2½ tablespoons chopped shallots

6 tablespoons white balsamic vinegar

1½ tablespoons soy sauce

1½ tablespoons ground white pepper

4 cooked Dungeness crabs, 2 pounds or
     larger if available

In a mixing bowl, combine the chili sauce, olive oil, garlic, shallots, vinegar, soy sauce, and white pepper, and mix well. Store this marinade in the refrigerator until needed.

Clean the crab thoroughly and crack each section of the legs and claws. This will ensure the marinade gets to all of the meat. Then marinate the crab overnight.

Place the crab with the marinade in a large sauté pan and put in the oven. Set on low broil and bake for 5 minutes. Another option is to grill the marinated crab on an outdoor grill, turning the crab pieces as they cook to avoid burning.

FLYING FISH

300 WESTLAKE AVENUE NORTH, SEATTLE
(206) 728-8595
WWW.FLYINGFISHRESTAURANT.COM
OWNER: CHRISTINE KEFF

Inspired during a trip to Thailand, where she tasted delicious fish grilled with flavorful ingredients, Chef Christine Keff was determined to open a restaurant serving simply prepared fresh fish. She succeeded, and sixteen years later, Keff's Flying Fish Restaurant continues to rank as a Seattle benchmark for outstanding seafood.

"I can't imagine doing anything else," says the James Beard Award–winning chef. "When you drop by the restaurant, I want you to have a good time."

And a good time customers like to have. Originally opened in Belltown, Flying Fish is now located on Westlake Avenue, offering contemporary decor in a much larger space. The theme is Northwest-inspired seafood—from locally sourced razor clams and troll-caught salmon, to pan fried sturgeon and rockfish that's fried whole. The fish is not only fresh but sustainable, and that's a big deal to Seattleites, who like to know where their food comes from and how it's harvested.

The Flying Fish bar is popular with the South Lake Union crowd, especially during happy hour. The restaurant offers two dozen different tequilas along with infused vodkas and seasonal cocktails. If you go, be sure to try the cucumber tequila with the Salt and Pepper Dungeness Crab. And don't forget dessert. They make a mean rhubarb pie topped with ginger ice cream.

CHEF CHRISTINE KEFF

LINGCOD IN KASU MARINADE

SERVES 4

For the Lingcod:

¼ cup kasu lees (available at specialty grocery
    stores and Asian markets), or light mayo
    and lemon pepper

1 tablespoon soy sauce

1 tablespoon mirin (sweet cooking wine)

1 tablespoon sake

2 tablespoons water

4 (6-ounce) pieces fresh Alaskan lingcod,
    1 to 2 inches thick

2 tablespoons canola oil

4 baby bok choy, steamed, optional

For the Broth:

1 cup chicken stock

1 tablespoon soy sauce

1 teaspoon dashi-no-moto powder
    (available at Asian markets)

1 teaspoon diced preserved lemon

1 teaspoon mirin

1 cup sake

Salt to taste

To prepare the lingcod: In a small bowl, combine
the kasu lees, soy sauce, mirin, sake, and water
and blend to a smooth paste. Coat the lingcod
and marinate for 2 hours in a glass bowl.

To make the broth: Combine the chicken stock,
soy sauce, dashi-no-moto powder, preserved
lemon, mirin, and sake in a small saucepan. Bring
to a boil, turn the heat down, and simmer for
5 minutes; season with salt.

To cook the lingcod: Heat the canola oil in a sauté
pan large enough to hold the 4 pieces of fish.
When the oil is shimmering, add the fish. Cook
over medium heat until the fish lifts away from the
pan. Turn the pieces over and finish cooking, until
the fish flakes.

To serve: Divide the lingcod among four shallow
bowls, such as soup plates, ladle the broth
around the fish, and serve with steamed baby
bok choy.

Lingcod Tacos

SERVES 6

1 tablespoon paprika

1 tablespoon cumin

1 teaspoon oregano

1 teaspoon chipotle flakes

½ teaspoon black pepper

¼ teaspoon white pepper

¼ teaspoon ground hot chile pepper

1 teaspoon garlic salt

1 tablespoon salt

2 pounds fresh Alaskan lingcod

Vegetable oil, for searing

Fresh guacamole

Fresh salsa

Warm tortillas (flour or corn)

In a mixing bowl combine the paprika, cumin, oregano, chipotle flakes, black and white pepper, ground chile, garlic salt, and salt, and mix thoroughly. Cut the fish into 2-inch cubes and sprinkle with enough spice mixture to thoroughly coat the fish.

In a large (12 inches or larger) sauté pan, heat enough oil to coat the bottom of the pan. When the oil is hot, add one-quarter of the fish cubes. Toss, browning on all sides, until the fish begins to flake. Transfer to a sheet pan and keep warm in a 150°F oven. Repeat the process with the rest of the fish, a quarter at a time.

Place the lingcod on a large serving platter, along with guacamole, your favorite salsa, and warm tortillas.

Rover's

2808 East Madison Street, Seattle
(206) 325-7442
WWW.THECHEFINTHEHAT.COM
Owner: Thierry Rautureau

If you're a foodie seeking fresh, organic Northwest ingredients prepared by a French culinary expert, head into Rover's on East Madison Street.

Chef Thierry Rautureau—known locally as the "Chef in the Hat," because of his signature fedora he wears everywhere—has been entertaining guests at Rover's for twenty-four years. Given a James Beard Award for "Best Chef in the Pacific Northwest," Chef Rautureau has found the perfect combination of French-inspired cuisine paired with excellent wines (from a list that features more than five hundred labels) amid an elegant-yet-relaxed atmosphere. He likes to refer to Rover's as the "neighborhood restaurant." What also makes Rover's unique is the a la carte menu, which is a nice alternative to other menus around town, especially for those liking to save a buck.

The Rover's recipes Chef Rautureau provides here emphasize one of the foods that put Seattle on the culinary map: fish. One preparation is largely Mediterranean, playing on the sunny and briny flavors of concentrated tomato, capers, olives, and mackerel. The other acknowledges Seattle's proximity to Asia, showcasing Japanese ingredients and flavors like tuna, wasabi, ginger, sesame oil, and soy sauce.

MACKEREL WITH TOMATO CONFIT &
CAPER VINAIGRETTE

SERVES 4

1 pound plum tomatoes, halved

Salt and freshly ground white pepper to taste

6–8 sprigs thyme

½ cup plus 1 tablespoon olive oil

8 large caper berries

8 large pitted black olives, quartered

8 large pitted green olives (such as picholine), quartered

1 tablespoon small "nonpareil" capers

4 teaspoons marine cider vinegar or white wine vinegar

2 teaspoons minced shallot

1 teaspoon minced chives

¼ teaspoon minced thyme

¼ teaspoon minced garlic

4 mackerel fillet pieces (about 4 ounces each)

2 teaspoons turmeric oil, optional

Fennel sprigs, for garnish

Minced chives, for garnish

Preheat the oven to 300°F.

To make the tomato confit: Set the tomato halves in a small roasting pan, cut side up, and season with salt and pepper. Top the tomatoes with thyme sprigs, drizzle ½ cup of the olive oil over, and bake until the tomatoes are very tender and aromatic, about 1¼ hours, turning the tomato halves after about 45 minutes and basting them with the oil 4 or 5 times during cooking. Set the pan of tomato confit aside on a wire rack to cool. Increase the oven temperature to 350°F.

To make the caper vinaigrette: Cut the caper berries just to one side of the stem so that the stem is fully attached to one half, and set the stemmed halves aside for garnish. Quarter the remaining halves and put them in a medium saucepan with the black and green olives and small capers. Add the vinegar, shallots, chives, thyme, and garlic. Drain ¼ cup of the tomato confit oil from the roasting pan and add the oil to the saucepan, with salt and pepper to taste. Toss well to evenly mix and set aside to marinate while cooking the mackerel.

To cook the fish: Heat a large ovenproof skillet over medium-high heat, then add the remaining 1 tablespoon of olive oil. Season the mackerel fillet pieces with salt and pepper and add them to the hot skillet, drizzling the turmeric oil around them, if desired. Brown the mackerel well on both sides, 2 to 3 minutes total, then transfer the skillet to the oven and bake until only a bit of translucence remains in the center, 3 to 4 minutes. Remove the skillet from the oven and carefully peel away the skin from the fillets and remove the dark band of flesh (which is quite strongly flavored) from just under the skin.

To serve: Gently warm the caper vinaigrette over medium-low heat, stirring to evenly mix, 2 to 3 minutes. Peel away and discard the skin from the tomato confit halves and lay 3 halves cut side down alongside each other in the center of warmed serving plates. Lay the mackerel on the tomatoes and spoon the warmed caper vinaigrette over the mackerel, drizzling the liquid over and around the fish. Top the fish with the reserved caper berry halves, add a few small fennel sprigs around the fish, sprinkle chives over all, and serve right away.

Tuna Sashimi with Sea Beans & Wasabi Sesame Dressing

SERVES 6

1 pound sashimi grade ahi tuna

2 teaspoons minced chives

1 teaspoon minced shallot

1 tablespoon plus 1 teaspoon sesame oil

¼ teaspoon grated ginger

¼ teaspoon minced garlic

Salt and freshly ground white pepper to taste

6 to 8 ounces sea beans (seeds and fruits that
    wash ashore; available at farmers' markets,
    fine grocery stores, and online)

2 tablespoons soy sauce

½ teaspoon wasabi powder

Basil oil or olive oil for garnish

Basil leaves for garnish

Cut 6 paper-thin slices of tuna to use as a garnish and set aside. Cut the remaining tuna into ¼-inch dice and place in a medium bowl. Add the chives, shallot, 1 teaspoon sesame oil, ginger, garlic, and salt and pepper and toss gently but thoroughly; set aside while preparing the sea beans.

Trim away any tough stems from the sea beans, saving only the tender parts. Bring a large saucepan of water (not salted) to a boil and prepare a bowl of ice water. Add the sea beans to the boiling water and cook until tender and bright green, 1 to 2 minutes. Drain and submerge into the ice water to quickly chill, then drain well again and lay the sea beans out on paper towels to dry.

Combine the soy sauce, remaining 1 tablespoon sesame oil, and wasabi in a medium bowl and whisk well to blend. Add the blanched sea beans and toss to evenly coat.

To serve: Use a slotted spoon to scoop out the sea beans and arrange in circles in the center of six serving plates, reserving the dressing. Lightly oil a 2-inch ring mold, if available, and set the mold on top of one of the sea bean circles. Spoon one-sixth of the diced tuna mixture into the mold and press down into an even disk with the back of the spoon (or simply spoon a tidy round of the tuna sashimi over the sea beans and use your fingers to form it into something of a cylinder). Lift off the ring and repeat with the remaining tuna. Drape the reserved slices of tuna around the outside of the tuna sashimi. Drizzle the reserved dressing and some basil oil or olive oil around the sea beans, top the tuna with a basil leaf, and serve right away.

TRELLIS RESTAURANT

220 KIRKLAND AVENUE, KIRKLAND
(425) 284-5900
WWW.HEATHMANKIRKLAND.COM
OWNER: THE PREFERRED HOTEL GROUP

Located inside the plush Four Diamond Heathman Hotel in Kirkland, Trellis Restaurant is a true farm-to-table experience—and one of the Eastside's best-kept secrets. That's because the fruits and vegetables, including thirty different kinds of heirloom tomatoes, are grown right on Executive Chef Brian Scheehser's farm. The restaurant's sustainable seafood and organic beef and poultry also come from local and reputable sources, ensuring the highest-quality meats possible.

To experience what freshness really tastes like, order the Two Hour Salad, which is made from ingredients that were handpicked within two hours from Chef Scheehser's farm. "I consider myself 50 percent chef and 50 percent farmer," admits Chef Scheehser, who also harvests his fields for such savory dishes as his vibrant Beet Salad, Stewed Farm Tomatoes and Onions, and Shaved Garden Zucchini, with fresh endive and roasted bell peppers also from the farm. Patrons dining at Trellis, whether inside or outside on the lovely heated patio, can also have the opportunity to experience and appreciate incredible organic entrees that are representative of the Northwest, like Lavender-Smoked Duck Breast, Brook Trout, and Roasted Pheasant.

And for those who enjoy happy hour, Trellis's open bar during "Crush Hour" is popular, especially for the urban mid-thirties and up crowd. The cocktails are equally as tempting as the food, so be sure to try a Boulevardier or Bombshell as you nibble on the house-made breadsticks.

Fresh Wild Alaskan Halibut with Shoestring Vegetables & Lemon-Herb Vinaigrette

SERVES 4

Lemon-Herb Vinaigrette:

4 teaspoons fresh lemon juice

¼ cup extra-virgin olive oil

1 medium shallot, peeled and cut into small dice

2 teaspoons capers

3 tablespoons chiffonade fresh basil

3 tablespoons chopped fresh Italian parsley

Salt and pepper to taste

Halibut:

1 teaspoon olive oil for searing

4 fillets (6 ounces each) fresh Alaskan Halibut

Shoestring Vegetables:

3 stalks celery

3 carrots, peeled

3 leeks

To make the vinaigrette: In a small bowl whisk together the lemon juice, olive oil, shallots, capers, basil, and parsley. Season to taste with salt and pepper. Reserve at room temperature.

To make the halibut: In a large sauté pan over medium-high heat, add the olive oil. Add the fish, taking caution not to splash the oil when putting the halibut in the pan. Sear 2 to 3 minutes on each side until golden brown.

To make the vegetables: Julienne the celery, carrots, and leeks. Add the vegetables to a pot of boiling water and blanch until just tender.

To serve: Place shoestring vegetables in the center of each serving plate. Place a halibut fillet on top of the vegetables and drizzle with the vinaigrette. Dust with salt and black pepper just before serving.

Pan-Seared Wild Salmon with Granny Smith Apples

SERVES 4

4 (6-ounce) wild salmon fillets
8 ounces apple wood smoking chips
1 quart (4 cups) apple cider
1 tablespoon olive oil
Salt and pepper to taste
2 Granny Smith apples, peeled, cored,
    quartered, and sliced
1 tablespoon butter
1 bunch wild watercress

To smoke the salmon: Place the salmon fillets on a cooking rack and place inside a cold outdoor grill.

Heat the apple wood chips over a gas flame in a smoking or cast-iron pan until the chips are three-quarters burnt or charred (this can be done only in a well-ventilated area or on a grill in open air). Put the fire out on the chips and then place them inside the cold grill with the salmon. Allow the chips to smoke for 5 to 7 minutes, "smoking" the salmon.

To make the apple cider reduction: In a pot over low heat, add the apple cider. Allow to reduce until the cider achieves a syrup-like consistency. Make sure to watch closely, as you do not want to burn the syrup. Remove from heat, cool, and reserve.

To cook the salmon: Heat a large ovenproof sauté pan over medium-high heat and add the olive oil. Remove the "smoked" salmon from the cold grill and season with salt and pepper. Add to the hot pan and sear skin side up until golden brown. Remove from heat and transfer the pan to a preheated 400°F oven. Finish cooking the salmon, approximately 5 minutes.

While the salmon is cooking, add the apples and butter to another sauté pan over medium heat and lightly sauté. Season with salt. The apples should be tender but not soft. Remove from heat and reserve.

To serve: Place a bed of the cooked apples on 4 serving plates. Add a small handful of watercress on top of the apples. Place a salmon fillet on top of the watercress and drizzle with the apple cider reduction. Serve immediately.

AQUA BY EL GAUCHO

FORMERLY WATERFRONT SEAFOOD GRILL

2801 ALASKAN WAY, PIER 70, SEATTLE
(206) 956-9171
WWW.WATERFRONTPIER70.COM
OWNER: PAUL MACKAY

When you're seated at a white-tablecloth waterfront table at the tip of Pier 70 at Aqua by El Gaucho, overlooking Elliott Bay and the beehive of boating activity, from the lone fisherman trolling for salmon to the massive Washington State ferries shuttling passengers to neighboring islands, you know you're in the perfect place. Inside tip: Some seating faces Seattle, so when making reservations request a waterfront view that faces Puget Sound. On summer nights the sunset is spectacular as the sun drops over the Olympic Mountains.

Aqua by El Gaucho, formerly named Waterfront Seafood Grill, offers not only stunning panoramic views but some of the best seafood in town. Owner Paul Mackay also operates the popular Seattle steakhouse El Gaucho.

Aqua by El Gaucho has been remodeled so patrons can now appreciate new booths and carpet while still enjoying an award-winning menu, which has remained virtually the same. That means you can still fight over the Stuffed Baja Prawns, the last spoonful of the rich and spicy Crab Bisque (note that the bisque is rich because it's made with Johnny Walker Red!), or the decadent Emerald City Volcano (Aqua's version of baked Alaska).

Like most of the popular restaurants in town, happy hour is equally encouraged at Aqua by El Gaucho. The bar can get packed, so arrive early or be patient. To take the edge off, try a Hemmingway Daiquiri or Joe's Sangria.

STUFFED PRAWNS WITH PIQUILLO PEPPER SAUCE

SERVES 4

2½ pounds fresh-picked Dungeness crabmeat

½ pound bay shrimp, peeled

2 cups mayonnaise

1½ tablespoons Old Bay seasoning

1 cup chopped fresh basil

1 teaspoon white pepper

¼ cup fresh lemon juice

1 cup chopped green onions

25 u-10 size fresh prawns, peeled and deveined

Olive oil

1 cup toasted bread crumbs

Piquillo Pepper Sauce (recipe below)

In a mixing bowl, combine the crabmeat, bay shrimp, mayonnaise, Old Bay seasoning, basil, white pepper, lemon juice, and green onions and mix well.

Butterfly the prawns, being careful not to separate the halves.

Lay the prawns out on a baking sheet rubbed with a little olive oil. Add a generous amount of the crabmeat stuffing to the prawns. Sprinkle the toasted bread crumbs on top of each prawn. Bake in a hot oven until the prawns are cooked and the bread crumb has some color. Remove from heat and serve with warm piquillo pepper sauce.

PIQUILLO PEPPER SAUCE

1 cup roasted tomatoes

4 ounces (½ cup) roasted piquillo peppers

1 tablespoon peeled and chopped shallots

1 tablespoon fresh lemon juice

2 ounces white balsamic vinegar

1 cup olive oil

¼ teaspoon cayenne

2 teaspoons kosher salt

½ bunch fresh cilantro, stems removed

Add all the ingredients to a blender and blend until smooth. Just before serving, gently heat the sauce in a saucepan over low to medium heat until warm.

Dungeness Crab Macaroni & Cheese
SERVES 4

1 live Dungeness crab, about 2 pounds

½ pound short noodle pasta, like elbow macaroni

1½ cups heavy cream

1 teaspoon kosher salt

½ teaspoon black pepper

¼ cup grated Parmigiana Reggiano

2 teaspoons butter

1 tablespoon black truffles, optional

2 teaspoons chopped chives

Boil the crab in salted water for 10 minutes, then remove from water. Let the crab rest on the counter for 5 minutes, then cool completely in ice water. Remove from the water and clean the crab, removing all the meat from the claws, legs, and back fin. Keep the meat chilled until ready to use.

Bring another pot of water seasoned with 2 tablespoons of salt to a boil. Add the pasta and cook until al dente. Try to time the cooking of the pasta with the reduction of the sauce. The pasta should take approximately 9 minutes once it begins to boil again.

Pour the cream into a heavy-bottom saucepan and reduce by two-thirds, which should take about 5 minutes (be sure the pan is large enough so the cream doesn't boil over). Season with salt and pepper and stir in the Parmigiana Reggiano and butter. Keep warm until ready to serve.

Add the pasta to the cream and cheese sauce and divide among serving plates or serve in a family-style bowl. Spoon the fresh-picked crabmeat over the top. Generously garnish with the chopped black truffles, if using, and chives. Enjoy while hot.

THE SEATTLE WATERFRONT

The Seattle Waterfront downtown is a premier tourist destination. A bustling and scenic 1.3-mile stretch along Alaskan Way, the best way to experience the sights, smells, and tastes of the Waterfront is on foot. The walk from end to end takes about thirty minutes. Along the way, stop and watch the Seattle ferries shuttle passengers to and from neighboring islands, visit the Seattle Aquarium, take a cruise on Puget Sound, buy a souvenir, and definitely poke your head into the world-famous Ye Old Curiosity Shop, where shrunken heads, a mermaid, and "Sylvester" the mummy are on display (but not for sale). There are plenty of restaurants and eateries along the Waterfront, all known for serving traditional Pacific Northwest seafood. Open-air vendors serve battered fish, fresh oysters, and hearty clam chowder daily. One of the best-known seafood stops is Ivar's, a Seattle favorite since 1938.

Beef, Lamb, Pork & Poultry

Dry-aged. Organic. Free range. Seattle has it covered when it comes to high-quality, naturally raised meats and poultry. Many local markets and butcher shops even make their own sausages without the use of nitrates, nitrites, phosphates, sugar, or MSG. If you've never tasted true free-range organic meats and poultry, you'll be amazed at the texture and flavor difference. In fact many restaurateurs are paying a little extra these days to make the commitment to offering their patrons the finest quality of meats and poultry.

Venetian-inspired Cicchetti Kitchen & Bar takes the stage with its often-requested beef brisket served with a generous helping of Greek creamed spinach. Neighborhood restaurant Coho Cafe takes a break from the local seafood scene to offer a mouthwatering Hawaiian favorite—Kogi Short Rib & Egg Stack. Seattle's El Gaucho, best known for its twenty-eight-day dry-aged certified angus beef prime steaks and *Wine Spectator*'s acknowledgment of the four-hundred-bottle wine list, reveals the coveted and always tasty chateaubriand accompanied by El Gaucho's cheese & beer sauce, elevating baked potatoes to a delicious new level. Not to be outclassed, The Metropolitan Grill—Seattle's dining mecca for steak lovers (and sports celebrities)—makes a rare appearance and delivers its prized rib eye with bourbon-braised onions and roasted garlic along with a grilled rack of lamb with zesty herb mint jus. Luc, a newcomer to the Seattle culinary scene, shows off its Moroccan-style leg of lamb and a grilled-to-perfection pork chop.

Pork is very popular in Seattle, especially with many neighboring farms, so Earth & Ocean and new chef Ryan Loo tempt carnivores with a braised pork belly dish. Vashon Island's very own Sea Breeze Farms and island eatery La Boucherie prefers to excite its guests with succulent organic pork chops with bacon brussels sprouts and a summer pork chop with grilled sweet corn polenta and salsa cotta.

And we cannot forget the chicken—the most widely consumed meat on the planet—so Palisade, one of Seattle's premier restaurants, revitalizes a classic favorite from the original 1992 Palisade menu by featuring a free range Macadamia Nut Chicken.

Cicchetti Kitchen & Bar

121 East Boston Street, Seattle
(206) 859-4155
www.serafinaseattle.com
Owner: Susan Kaufman

Cicchetti, with its backlit bar, vaulted beam ceiling, and contemporary design, is the romantic-yet-trendy sister restaurant to owner Susan Kaufman's Serafina, which is tucked around the corner.

Anchored by Executive Chef Dylan Giordan and located in the charming Eastlake neighborhood, Cicchetti is a much more casual and laid-back version of Serafina and is best known for its Mediterranean food—both hot and cold—which is typically shared tapas style. Locals favor the Venetian Marinated Mussels, Grilled Halloumi with Spicy Marinated Watermelon, and the wood-fired Pizza Margherita. The dishes are often light and perfectly proportioned and offer the perfect blend of flavor combinations, including drizzles of real truffle oil.

Happy hour at Cicchetti is also a hit with the community, with discounted cocktails and tasty Truffle Popcorn to snack on. The bar does get crowded, so don't be afraid to step outside onto the deck (weather permitting) for some fresh air and a beautiful view of Lake Union. The bartenders at Cicchetti are friendly no matter what hour of the day and will even take a moment to educate you on the various spirits and signature drinks available—because with names like Nahal Hemel, Safranbolu, and a Mitzvot, you just may want to consult the bartender.

Tomato Braised Beef Brisket with Greek-Style Creamed Spinach

SERVES 6

Beef Brisket:

4 pounds beef brisket, trimmed and
   cut into 8-ounce portions
Salt and pepper to taste
3 tablespoons olive oil
2 medium yellow onions, peeled and diced
1 cup peeled garlic cloves
¼ cup oregano leaves (less 2 tablespoons
   reserved for spinach recipe)
2 cups white wine
8 cups peeled tomatoes (such as San Marzano),
   crushed by hand and the liquid reserved

Spinach:

1 cup chopped leek, soaked in water
3 tablespoons olive oil, divided
2 pinches salt, divided
1 pound fresh spinach
1 lemon, zested
2 tablespoons oregano leaves (reserved
   from brisket recipe)
2 cups crumbled feta cheese
3 cups Greek-style plain yogurt

To make the beef brisket: Season the brisket well with salt and pepper. Cover in plastic wrap and refrigerate for 24 hours.

Preheat the oven to 325°F. In a Dutch oven, heat the olive oil and carefully add 8 ounces brisket; cook until well browned on all sides, then remove from the Dutch oven. Work in 8-ounce batches and be careful not to overcrowd the pot. When all the beef pieces have been nicely browned, add the onions to the pot and stir. Sauté on medium heat for 5 minutes.

Meanwhile, roughly chop the garlic and add to the pot. Add all but 2 tablespoons oregano leaves to the onions and garlic, along with the white wine. Cook until the wine has evaporated, about 5 minutes. Add the crushed tomatoes and their liquid. Bring to a boil, check for seasoning and add salt and pepper to taste, add the beef, and stir to cover. Place the Dutch oven in the oven for 3½ hours, or until the beef is very tender.

To make the spinach: In a 4-quart pot over low heat, sweat the leeks with 1 tablespoon olive oil and a pinch of salt. The leeks will slowly release their moisture and concentrate their sweetness. When the leeks are fully translucent, add the spinach, another 2 tablespoons olive oil, and another generous pinch of salt, and stir. The spinach will cook down; continue to cook until the moisture that exudes from the spinach has evaporated and the spinach is soft. Then add the lemon zest, remaining oregano, feta, and yogurt. Cook slowly until the flavors combine, about 5 minutes.

To serve: Divide the spinach among six warmed wide bowls. Place a portion of brisket in each bowl and top each with a couple spoonfuls of tomato braising liquid.

COHO CAFÉ RESTAURANT & BAR

6130 EAST LAKE SAMMAMISH PARKWAY SOUTHEAST, ISSAQUAH
(425) 391-4040
WWW.COHOCAFE.COM
OWNERS: STEVE PRICE AND ARNIES RESTAURANT NW

Not all restaurants have to be elegant, expensive, and written up in multiple magazines to be good. One family-oriented eatery that believes in offering exciting food at attractive prices—a positive in today's sluggish economy—is the Coho Café Restaurant & Bar. With locations in Issaquah and Redmond, Coho, like its name implies, serves up locally caught Northwest seafood, such as fresh wild salmon and Dungeness crab, along with a bevy of meats, poultry, salads, vegetable dishes, and desserts where even the ice cream is brought in from a local creamery.

The menu is extensive, so take your time perusing it, as there is plenty to choose from to satisfy everyone's craving. If you arrive on a Monday, wines are half price.

The executive chefs at both locations are equally skilled, so expect consistent food. Coho Redmond chef, Jacob Nyman, is a graduate of the New England Culinary Institute. His culinary background speaks for itself: He held the senior executive sous chef position at Kincaid's in San Francisco and the executive chef position at Palomino in Honolulu. He was also on the corporate transition team for Ruth's Chris in Seattle and Bellevue. An avid fisherman, Chef Nyman incorporates local fresh seafood and other local ingredients into many of his signature dishes.

Coho's Issaquah head chef, Bruce Nacion, has spent his life working his way to the top through the kitchens of some of the finest restaurants in Hawaii. His talent and exposure to many cultures and styles of cooking have given him the ability to put wonderful twists on traditional cuisine. The Kogi Short Rib & Egg Stack recipe featured here is his twist on a local Hawaiian favorite, Loco Moco. "It's a fun dish that's easy to make at home," says Chef Nacion. "It's also an attractive dish, so plating is important, because visual presentation is everything."

KOGI SHORT RIB & EGG STACK

SERVES 4

Kim Chee Fried Rice Cake:

¾ cup calrose rice (or any variety of
   medium-grain white rice)

1 cup water

2 teaspoons vegetable oil, divided

1 egg, lightly beaten

1 teaspoon sesame oil

2 ounces bacon, cut into ¼-inch dice

3 tablespoons diced celery

1¼ ounce peeled and diced carrots

1¼ ounce peeled and diced onion

1 teaspoon peeled and minced garlic

5 teaspoons sambal olek (chili paste), available
   at Asian markets and supermarkets

5 teaspoons oyster sauce

¼ teaspoon white pepper

¼ teaspoon kosher salt

¼ teaspoon black pepper

1½ teaspoons thinly sliced green onions

¼ cup plus 1 tablespoon chopped medium-hot
   kim chee (available at Asian markets)

Cilantro Oil:

1½ teaspoons stemmed and chopped
   fresh cilantro

¼ cup vegetable oil

½ teaspoon fresh lemon juice

1 pinch kosher salt

Braised Kalbi Beef Short Ribs:

2 pounds (3-inch cut) boneless beef short ribs

Salt and pepper to taste

1 cup chicken broth

1 cup beef broth

Kalbi Sauce:

¼ cup plus 1 tablespoon soy sauce

½ teaspoon peeled and minced garlic

¼ teaspoon peeled and minced ginger

2 teaspoons thinly sliced green onion

1/3 cup sugar

1/8 teaspoon black pepper

1 teaspoon sesame seeds, toasted

1/8 teaspoon crushed red pepper flakes

1 teaspoon sesame oil

1 teaspoon vegetable oil

Final Assembly:

Vegetable oil, as needed

8 eggs

To make the kim chee fried rice cake: Place the
rice and water in a covered saucepan and cook
until just done. Spread out the cooked rice on a
plate to cool completely. (This can be done a day
ahead.)

Place 1 teaspoon of the vegetable oil in a sauté
pan, add the egg and cook scrambled. Remove
from heat and set aside.

Next, heat the sesame oil and the remaining
1 teaspoon vegetable oil in a large pot over
medium heat. Add the bacon and cook until
brown but not crispy. Add the celery, carrots,
onions, and garlic and cook until translucent. Add
the cooked rice and stir-fry until heated through.
Add the sambal olek, oyster sauce, white pepper,
salt, and black pepper and combine. Remove
from heat and add the green onions, kim chee,
and the scrambled egg. Combine thoroughly. Let
the mixture cool to room temperature.

When cool, scoop 6-ounce (¾ cup) balls of the fried rice mixture and form four round cakes about 3½ inches in diameter and ¾-inch thick each. Place on a plate wrapped in plastic wrap and cool in the refrigerator for later use.

To make the cilantro oil: Combine the cilantro, vegetable oil, lemon juice, and kosher salt in a blender. Puree until the cilantro is minced very fine. Set aside.

To make the braised kalbi beef short ribs: Preheat the oven to 350°F. Season the short ribs with salt and pepper. Preheat a sauté pan on high heat, add the ribs, and sear on all sides. Remove the ribs and place them in a deep baking dish.

Meanwhile, in a saucepan bring the chicken broth and beef broth to a boil. Pour the hot broth over the short ribs and submerge the ribs. Cover the dish with foil and place in the oven for about 3 hours, or until the meat is fork tender.

To make the kalbi sauce: Combine the soy sauce, garlic, ginger, green onion, sugar, black pepper, sesame seeds, crushed red pepper, and the sesame and vegetable oils in a bowl and whisk to blend.

Remove the short ribs from the braising liquid and lay out on a baking pan. Drizzle about half of the kalbi sauce over the cooked short ribs and reserve the rest for plating the dish. Divide the short ribs into four equal portions. Keep the short ribs warm in the oven while you finish preparing the dish.

The final assembly: Preheat a large nonstick griddle over medium heat. Heat 2 tablespoons vegetable oil in the griddle and sear the rice cakes until they are nicely brown on one side. Flip and repeat on the other side. Cook the cakes until heated through and slightly crispy, then remove and keep warm in the oven with the short ribs.

Dip four egg rings lightly in vegetable oil and place on the heated griddle. Then crack 2 eggs in each ring. Cook sunny side up until the whites are just set. Then remove the rings.

To serve: Place a seared rice cake in the center of each serving plate. Place a portion of the short ribs on each rice cake, making a relatively even layer. Carefully place 2 fried eggs on top of each short rib portion to create a 3-layer stack. Drizzle the top of each stack with about 1 tablespoon of both the kalbi sauce and cilantro oil. Serve immediately.

To make this dish, you will need four silicone egg rings. These can be found at kitchen stores and online.

EL GAUCHO

2505 FIRST AVENUE, SEATTLE
(206) 728-1337
WWW.ELGAUCHO.COM
OWNER: PAUL MACKAY

Every big city seems to have its celebrated steak house. In Seattle, one of the favorites is the classy and swanky El Gaucho, which happens to be the official steak house of the Seattle Seahawks and the Seattle Sounders sports teams.

Inside the roomy dimly lit space (yes, you really do get handed a mini flashlight to see the menu), anchored by heavy wood and furniture, it's apparent at first glance El Gaucho caters to the elite meat-and-potatoes crowd. Suits and ties and evening gowns are typically the norm here, so if you feel like dressing up for a culinary adventure you're sure to remember, this is a great place to spend it.

Reservations are definitely a must, as El Gaucho fills up nightly. If you happen to be stumbling in off the street, head for the bar, which serves the same menu as the expansive dining room but in a more casual atmosphere. There are often seats available, and the service is just as good.

The food, without question, is magnificent, and definitely worth the high price. From the steak tartare and Caesar salad—both prepared tableside—to the carved tableside porterhouse and Chateaubriand (the Chateau recipe is featured here), El Gaucho sets the bar high; it's clear why it is one of America's best steak houses. And if you do spring for the pricey cuts of dry-aged beef, be sure to order a shareable side like the lobster mashed potatoes or an entire grilled Portobello mushroom.

After dinner don't forget to check out the piano bar or cigar room (which includes a cigar menu), where both signature and classic cocktails are served.

El Gaucho also has locations in Bellevue, Tacoma, and Portland, Oregon.

CHATEAUBRIAND

SERVES 4

Chateaubriand:

2½–3 pounds beef tenderloin, trimmed

2 teaspoons steak seasoning

4 tablespoons softened butter, optional

1 teaspoon dry mustard

Sautéed Mushrooms:

¼ cup extra-virgin olive oil

½ lemon, juiced

¼ teaspoon kosher salt

¼ teaspoon ground black pepper

12 crimini mushrooms

1 tablespoon softened butter

¼ cup white wine

½ teaspoon minced fresh garlic

Broiled Tomatoes:

2 beefsteak or heirloom tomatoes

Salt and pepper to taste

4 tablespoons grated Reggiano cheese

Asparagus:

¾ pound fresh asparagus

Olive oil or melted butter to finish

Salt and pepper to taste

Cliff Sauce:

½ teaspoon Worcestershire sauce

2 tablespoons softened butter

1 tablespoon red wine, heated slightly to melt the butter

¼ cup meat drippings (juice and solids from the pan)

To make the chateaubriand: Thoroughly season the meat with steak seasoning, and then grill over medium heat on all four sides until desired degree of doneness—about 20 to 25 minutes for medium rare (internal temperature 115°F) and 30 to 35 minutes for well done (150°F), depending on the meat's thickness. (Charcoal grills cook faster than gas grills, so be careful not to char the meat or you will have a difficult time penetrating the inside.) While the meat cooks, prepare the vegetables and Cliff Sauce. When meat is finished cooking, remove from the heat and let stand 2 to 3 minutes. Top with the softened butter to create a richer sauce, if desired. Spread the dry mustard on top of the cooked meat. Collect the juices from the meat and reserve them to make the Cliff Sauce.

To make the mushrooms: Combine the olive oil, lemon juice, salt, and pepper. Add the mushrooms and let marinate for at least 15 to 20 minutes. Transfer the marinated mushrooms to a hot grill and cook for about 1 minute on each side, to get a smoky flavor and grill marks, and then remove from the heat. Place the mushrooms in a sauté pan over medium heat along with the butter, white wine, and garlic. Stir often for 3 to 4 minutes. Keep warm until ready to serve.

To make the tomatoes: Cut the tomatoes in half and lay them cut side up. Sprinkle with salt and pepper and top each with about 2 tablespoons grated Reggiano cheese. Place under the broiler, about 4 inches from the heat. Broil for 4 to 6 minutes.

To make the asparagus: Remove an inch or two of stem from the asparagus, then steam, broil, or grill the spears. (To grill, do so for about 4 to 6 minutes alongside the meat when the meat is almost done.) After cooking, brush the asparagus with melted butter or olive oil and season with salt and pepper just before serving.

To make the Cliff Sauce: Combine the Worcestershire, butter, red wine, and meat drippings in a sauté pan or small bowl and whisk until smooth. Pour the sauce over the sliced meat or serve it on the side in a saucer.

As a suggested plating, place the mushrooms along the back edge of a large platter, place the tenderloin in front of the mushrooms, arrange the asparagus on the outer edge of both sides of the tenderloin, place 2 broiled tomatoes next to each portion of asparagus. Top the meat with the Cliff Sauce, if desired, or serve it on the side. Serve chateaubriand alongside baked potatoes topped with Gaucho Cheese & Beer Sauce, on the next page.

El Gaucho recommends using two pieces of meat to make cooking easier; ask the butcher for barrel-cut pieces of tenderloin—the thickest part of the muscle that has no connective tissue—which will make for a very tender steak.

Because of its thickness, cooking chateaubriand requires care to avoid overcooking the outside while leaving the center raw. For this purpose it is best to grill or roast the meat in a hot oven until it reaches an internal temperature of 130°F, which, after a short rest, will produce a medium-rare chateaubriand.

GAUCHO CHEESE & BEER SAUCE

2 teaspoons salad oil or canola oil

2 teaspoons butter

1 tablespoon minced green onions

½ tablespoon minced fresh Italian parsley

⅛ cup all-purpose flour

1 quart homogenized milk, heated to 100°F degrees

⅔ cup light beer, heated to 100°F degrees
     (Hefeweizen works well)

⅛ teaspoon granulated garlic

⅛ teaspoon cayenne pepper

¼ teaspoon kosher salt

1 pinch ground white pepper

1 pound cheddar cheese, grated

¼ teaspoon Worcestershire sauce

⅛ teaspoon dry mustard

Heat the oil and butter in a stockpot over medium heat. Add the green onions and parsley and sauté for 2 minutes. Add the flour to make a roux (paste-like consistency). Whisk until smooth and continue to cook for 30 minutes at the lowest heat possible, whisking every 5 minutes.

Turn off the heat and add the heated milk and beer, stirring to fully incorporate the liquids. (Using cold milk or beer makes the sauce lumpy. Be sure to heat these liquids before adding them to the roux.) When the mixture is smooth, return it to medium heat and whisk until it comes to a boil. Add the garlic, cayenne pepper, salt, and pepper and return to a boil. Reduce the heat to low and whisk continually for 5 to 10 minutes, until the sauce achieves a gravylike thickness. Remove from heat and add the cheddar cheese, Worcestershire, and dry mustard, stirring to prevent clumping, until smooth. Reserve the sauce until the meat is ready and serve over freshly baked potatoes.

METROPOLITAN GRILL

820 2ND AVENUE, SEATTLE
(206) 624-3287
WWW.THEMETROPOLITANGRILL.COM
OWNER: CONSOLIDATED RESTAURANTS INC.

The Metropolitan Grill—simply referred to as "the Met" by locals—has been serving up some of the most talked about steaks in downtown Seattle for years. Whether you dine in the lively bar accented with checkered flooring, marble, and hand-painted cocktail art, or the adjacent dining room furnished with cozy booths rich in mahogany and brass, the experience will be memorable.

Before taking your seat, take a moment to peruse the many familiar faces hanging on the lobby walls. From Jay Leno to Alex Rodriguez, lots of big-name celebrities have all eaten here. Also on display are the various cuts of corn-fed beef, so you'll have a better idea of what to order. The filet mignon remains the most requested, followed by the New York, porterhouse, and the chef's favorite, the Delmonico. But for a real treat, order the Chateaubriand for two. The cut is carved tableside and the accompanying Cliff Sauce is mixed right in front of you, made to your specifications. Don't forget to order a Dungeness Crab Claw Cocktail as an appetizer. The Met uses only the largest

pieces of leg meat. Other dish recommendations include the Iceberg Wedge with Rogue River Blue Cheese and a bowl of Maine Lobster Bisque made with a fine cognac.

Here, Executive Chef Eric Hellner features Snake River Farms Rib Eye with Bourbon-Braised Onions and Roasted Garlic. The distinctive American Wagyu Natural Beef from Snake River Farms is the foundation for the most remarkable steak experience. The exceptional tenderness and exquisite flavor of the beef are complemented with the caramelized sweetness of onions braised with Maker's Mark bourbon. Chef Hellner also presents the Met's Grilled Rack of Lamb with Herb Mint Jus. Like the Met's rack of lamb that is carved tableside for two, this recipe highlights the meat's juicy, succulent, and tender texture. The lamb is finished with veal demi and plated over polenta alongside seasoned grilled asparagus.

RIB EYE WITH BOURBON-BRAISED ONIONS & ROASTED GARLIC

SERVES 4

1 teaspoon granulated garlic

1 granulated onion

3 tablespoons kosher salt

1 teaspoon freshly ground black pepper

3 pounds rib eye steak or New York steak, cut into
    ¾-pound steaks about 1–1½ inches thick

Maker's Mark Bourbon–Braised Onions & Roasted
    Garlic (recipe below)

Preheat an outdoor grill to medium-high heat
(make sure to clean the grill and spray with a
nonstick cooking spray). Next, mix the granulated
garlic, onion, salt, and black pepper in a small
bowl.

Season the steaks evenly on all sides. Place
on the grill. Cook each side of the steaks for
approximately 5 to 6 minutes, turning 45 degrees
halfway through. (This is for a medium-rare steak;
always check with a meat thermometer to make
sure the steaks do not overcook.) Remove the
steaks from the grill at 115°F and allow to rest for
5 minutes. The steaks will continue to cook while
resting and should be about 120°F when ready
to serve.

Serve steaks with a side of Maker's Mark
Bourbon–Braised Onions & Roasted Garlic and
your favorite starch or vegetable.

MAKER'S MARK BOURBON–BRAISED ONIONS & ROASTED GARLIC

½ stick unsalted butter

3 pounds Walla Walla sweet onions,
    peeled and julienned

1 tablespoon salt

½ teaspoon black pepper

1 cup garlic cloves, roasted

1 cup packed brown sugar

½ cup Maker's Mark bourbon

½ cup au jus (store bought)

In a heavy-gauge stainless or copper pot, heat
the butter until melted. Add the onions, salt, and
pepper. Sauté until the onions are caramelized.
Add the garlic and brown sugar and toss to
combine. Add the bourbon. Burn off the alcohol
and reduce by 75 percent. Add the au jus and
cook to blend the flavors. Transfer to a serving
dish and serve alongside the steaks.

GRILLED RACK OF LAMB WITH HERB MINT JUS

SERVES 4

2 (28-ounce) 8-bone lamb racks
Salt and pepper to taste

Polenta:

½ cup chicken broth
½ cup heavy cream
Salt and pepper to taste
½ cup polenta
1 cup grated Parmesan cheese

Olive oil to grill asparagus
¾ pound asparagus

Veal Demi:

6 ounces veal demi-glace (store bought)
Water, as needed to achieve desired consistency
1 bunch fresh mint, chopped
Salt and pepper to taste

To prepare the lamb: Season the lamb racks with salt and pepper. Place on a grill over medium heat and mark all sides, then transfer to a preheated 350°F oven for 8 to 10 minutes, or until lamb reaches an internal temperature of 120°F degrees—for medium. Cook longer if desired.

To prepare the polenta: Begin the polenta while the lamb racks are finishing in the oven. In a large saucepan, combine the chicken broth and heavy cream. Bring to a boil over high heat. Add the salt, pepper, and polenta. Reduce heat to low and cook polenta until it is soft and has absorbed all the liquid. Fold in the cheese. Keep warm until ready to serve.

Next, lightly oil the asparagus and place on a hot grill. Grill until desired doneness.

To prepare the demi-glace: Combine the demi-glace, water, mint, salt, and pepper in a heavy saucepan. Bring to a slow simmer over medium-high heat. Allow to simmer to infuse the flavors into the sauce. Keep warm until ready to serve.

To serve: When the lamb is finished, remove from the oven. Divide 2 cups of the polenta and the asparagus among 4 serving plates. Cut the lamb racks into 4 equal pieces and plate. Finish with a drizzle of the veal demi. Serve immediately.

THE METROPOLITAN GRILL

The moment you step inside the Metropolitan Grill you'll see framed photographs of famous actors, sports heroes, and politicians adorning the walls, but not in a pretentious manner. After glancing at the many notable faces, you may quickly assume you're in good company . . . as everyone you're staring at also dined here! Some of the more prominent names include actor Michael Douglas, comedians Jay Leno and Robin Williams, country music legend Kenny Rogers, Amazon founder Jeff Bezos, and sports superstars Mike Ditka, Ken Griffey Jr., Alex Rodriguez, Shaquille O'Neal, and Joe Theismann. Unlike notable celebrity eateries like Hollywood's Spago, looky loos probably won't catch a glimpse of a famous face dining at the Met. Three private rooms, including one with its own private entrance and restroom, allow celebrities to slip in and out unbeknownst to guests in the main dining room and bar area.

LUC

2800 EAST MADISON STREET, SEATTLE
(206) 328-6645
WWW.THECHEFINTHEHAT.COM
OWNER: THIERRY RAUTUREAU

Next to his sister restaurant Rover's in Madison Park, Chef Thierry Rautureau (better known as the "Chef in the Hat") welcomes foodies to Luc, named after the chef's father. Flower arrangements courtesy of the chef's wife (a florist) complement the warm and homey paintings and decor, and a portrait paying homage to the restaurant's namesake adds a nice touch to a restaurant that wants you to feel relaxed and as though you're dining at home.

Better described as a neighborhood bistro where the dishes are more casual and less expensive than the upscale Rover's, Luc is a fun, friendly place to unwind, have a cocktail, and enjoy a delicious meal.

Chef Rautureau incorporates his French background into the French-American menu, with dishes such as French onion soup, Luc's famed burger with tomato jam and a side of the highly touted soufflé potato crisps, a pulled-pork BLT, and beef bourguignon stew. Come in for Luc's daily happy hour and snack on wonderfully prepared plates at special prices while sipping interesting cocktail combinations from the bar, such as a Mini Mad Hat'n and a Tini Lucatini. After all, Seattle is a city that loves its cocktails.

The two Luc recipes featured here are both grilled. The Grilled Leg of Lamb, prepared Moroccan style, is served with couscous and makes a magnificent centerpiece for any feast with family or friends. The Grilled Pork Chops with Dijon Mustard, Asparagus & Walla Walla Sweets is the perfect dish for any sunny spring evening.

GRILLED LEG OF LAMB MOROCCAN STYLE

SERVES 8–10

2 cups pitted and chopped green and black olives

4 tablespoons chopped shallots

1 tablespoon chopped garlic

3 teaspoons harissa (add more for a spicier result)

3 red bell peppers, roasted, skinned, and cut into small dice

1 teaspoon chopped fresh thyme

1 tablespoon chopped fresh chives

¾ cups Moroccan olive oil

Salt and pepper to taste

1 leg of lamb, about 3 pounds (deboned and butterflied)

In a salad bowl, combine the olives, shallots, garlic, harissa, red bell peppers, thyme, chives, olive oil, salt, and pepper. Spread half of this tapenade mixture on top of the lamb meat, patting gently. Turn the meat and spread the remaining tapenade on the other side. Let the meat marinate for at least 1½ hours.

Start the grill with all the coals in the center. When the coals are hot, move them to the side, close the lid, and get the grill extremely hot.

Place the lamb in the middle of the grill on the skin side first. Once marked, turn over and repeat the searing and close the lid of the grill to finish cooking. Once the meat is pink, or about 120°F, remove and let rest for about 30 minutes before slicing. Rewarm the sliced meat for a minute or two if necessary, then serve.

Great side dishes for this course include couscous, roasted garlic toast, and harissa sauce.

GRILLED PORK CHOP WITH DIJON MUSTARD, ASPARAGUS & WALLA WALLA SWEETS

SERVES 4

Pork Chops:

4 tablespoons Dijon mustard

2 tablespoons water

2 tablespoons olive oil

Ground black peppercorns to taste

4 pork chops, about 6 to 7 ounces each,
    with bone

Asparagus & Walla Walla Sweets:

16 medium to large asparagus stalks, peeled

4 tablespoons extra-virgin olive oil, divided

1 tablespoon chopped fresh thyme, divided

1 tablespoon kosher salt, divided

4 medium onions, peeled and halved,
    cut 2-inches high from bulb

To make the pork chops: In a mixing bowl combine the mustard and water, then whisk in the olive oil. Add the peppercorns. Whisk again to combine, then spread the mixture on both sides of the pork chops. Let sit in a pan to marinate in the refrigerator for at least 2 to 3 hours but no more than 8 hours.

Remove the chops from the refrigerator at least 1 hour before cooking.

To make the asparagus & Walla Walla sweets: At least 2 hours prior to cooking, mix together the asparagus, half the olive oil, half the thyme, and half the salt in a shallow pan. In a separate shallow pan, repeat with the onions.

Prepare the grill (coal and indirect heat is preferred) and let the heat rise to 425°F. Place the vegetables in the center and grill until cooked, and then place in a shallow pan and set aside. Clean the grill with a brush and place the chops in the middle of the grill. Cook for 5 to 7 minutes to mark and color, then turn on the other side and repeat the cooking method. Check for doneness (if using a meat thermometer, it should register 140°F).

To serve: Place a pork chop in the center of each plate, accompanied by the vegetables around the chop. Serve hot.

EARTH & OCEAN

1112 4TH AVENUE, SEATTLE
(206) 264-6060
WWW.EARTHOCEAN.NET
OWNERS: STARWOOD HOTELS AND RESORTS WORLDWIDE INC.

Located inside the fashionable W Hotel on 4th Avenue in the heart of downtown Seattle is the elegant-yet-contemporary Earth & Ocean Restaurant. Ardent supporters of the environment by serving clean foods that are good for you, Earth & Ocean Restaurant offers plenty of fresh sustainable seafood on the menu—like the local Penn Cove clams and wild sea bass—along with organic meats and the freshest Northwest fruits and vegetables from nearby farms.

Executive Chef Ryan Loo helms the kitchen at Earth & Ocean, having left the islands of Hawaii for life in Seattle. What makes Chef Loo excel at this popular establishment is his commitment to using fresh wholesome Northwest ingredients, for which Seattle is well recognized. Earth & Ocean enjoys serving power lunches to the downtown business crowd, so if you plan to drop in around the noon hour, be prepared for rush-hour traffic inside the restaurant. No wonder Earth & Ocean offers a "Rush Hour" menu, complete with "Rush Hour Specials."

Chef Loo is also in charge of the lively W Bar, which means you'll find fun and savory items on the menu including Sexy Fries and Curried Scallops. You can also experience

freshly made fruit-laden cocktails like a Bird of Paradise with fresh orange and pineapple juice, or a Skinny Lemonade made with acai and lemons fresh from the garden. If you order the Treetini, a fun cocktail shaken with acai, mint, and agave nectar, the restaurant will plant a tree in your honor. Now how's that for giving back to the environment?

Braised Pork Belly with Anson Mills Rosemary Polenta & Pomegranates

SERVES 6

Brine:

1 gallon (16 cups) cold water

1 medium onion, peeled and chopped

1 carrot, peeled and chopped

1 teaspoon cloves

1 leek, cleaned and chopped

1 celery rib, cleaned and chopped

2 cloves garlic, peeled

½ cup sugar

1 cup sea salt

½ tablespoon black peppercorns

1 tablespoon juniper berries

1 bay leaf

Pork Belly:

1–2 pounds slab pork belly (about 8 x 8-inch square, or as close to that as possible)

Salt and pepper to taste

1 onion, peeled and diced

1 carrot, peeled and diced

1 celery rib, diced

2 apples, diced

2 cups white wine

½ gallon (8 cups) chicken stock

1 sprig fresh rosemary

Rosemary Polenta:

¼ cup peeled and diced onion

1 tablespoon peeled and minced garlic

½ tablespoon olive oil

2½ cups milk

2½ cups water

2 cups polenta

½ cup grated fresh Parmesan

½ cup heavy cream (a bit more may be needed)

1 tablespoon chopped fresh rosemary

Pomegranate Syrup:

2 pomegranates, seeds only

¾ cup sugar

1 tablespoon salt, plus more to taste

1 teaspoon chopped fresh tarragon

2 tablespoons Grenache vinegar

1½ cups red wine vinegar

1½ cups pomegranate juice

Braising Greens:

2 tablespoons extra-virgin olive oil

1 pound braising greens (escarole leaves)

Squeeze of fresh lemon juice

Salt and pepper to taste

Garnish:

Lemon threads

Parsley leaves

To make the brine: Place all the brine ingredients in a large stockpot over medium heat. Bring to a quick simmer, then remove from heat. Allow to cool completely; do not strain.

To make the pork belly: Wash the pork belly with warm water and pierce several times with a fork over the entire surface. This will allow the brine to easily penetrate the belly.

Once the brine is cold, submerge the belly in it so it is completely covered, and then place into the refrigerator for no less than 24 hours.

The next day remove the belly from the brine, pat dry, and discard the brine. Season the belly with salt and pepper. Heat a large ovenproof sauté pan over high heat and add the belly. Sear on both sides until nicely browned; remove from heat and set aside.

In the same sauté pan, add the onions, carrots, celery, and apples. Sauté for a few minutes to begin browning the vegetables. Deglaze the pan with the white wine and allow the wine to reduce by half at a simmer. Once reduced, add the chicken stock and rosemary sprig and bring back to a simmer. Return the belly to the pan, cover with a tight-fitting lid, and place in a 375°F preheated oven. Allow the belly to braise until tender but not falling apart. This should take about 1½ hours.

Remove the belly from the braising liquid, strain the liquid and set aside for another purpose or discard. Portion the belly into 6 equal blocks or rectangles and set in a warm place until ready to serve.

To make the rosemary polenta: Sauté the onion and garlic in the olive oil over medium heat. Add the milk and water, bring to a simmer, then drizzle in the polenta, stirring constantly. Reduce the heat to a simmer and cook, stirring every 10 minutes until the polenta is soft and thick.

(Note: If using Anson Mills polenta, the cooking time will take about 2 hours, and additional stirring and stock may be needed during the cooking time.) Just before serving, add the cheese, cream, and rosemary. Stir to combine. The polenta should hold its shape but still be soft when ready to serve.

To make the pomegranate syrup: In a saucepan over low heat, combine the pomegranate seeds, sugar, salt, tarragon, vinegars, and half the pomegranate juice. Bring to a simmer and cook slowly until the seeds release their juices, about 20 minutes. Transfer the contents to a blender and blend until smooth. Strain and discard the pulp. Add the remaining pomegranate juice to the strained mixture and return to a simmer and further reduce until thickened, about another 20 minutes. Adjust the seasoning with salt, as needed. Set aside in a warm location until needed.

To make the braising greens: Heat a sauté pan with the olive oil until just hot. Add the clean escarole leaves and sauté until tender, about 3 minutes. Season with lemon juice, salt, and pepper.

To serve: Spoon a portion of the polenta in the center of each serving plate, and then place the sautéed escarole in a nice bundle in the center of the polenta. With a very sharp knife, slice the pork belly into 5¼-inch pieces and fan them over the escarole. Using a spoon, drizzle the pomegranate syrup over and around the pork belly, allowing drips and smears onto the plate. Garnish with a small salad of lemon threads and picked parsley leaves.

La Boucherie & Sea Breeze Farm on Vashon Island

17635 100th Avenue Southwest, Vashon
(206) 567-4628
WWW.SEABREEZEFARM.NET
Owners: George and Kristin Page

Catch a Seattle ferry to neighboring Vashon Island and you'll experience true farm-to-table cuisine at the quaint La Boucherie nestled on a peaceful little street corner.

Owners George and Kristin Page opened the restaurant—which includes a butcher shop—in 2008, when the couple decided to showcase the many organic and artisan products from their private farm located only minutes away.

Visit the Pages' Sea Breeze Farm and you'll marvel at the small-scale yet extremely efficient family-run operation. Cattle, chickens, ducks, and geese graze and free range outside. Wine barrels doubling as smokers fill the air with tempting aromas as some of the best-tasting hams are prepared, using the Pages' fat-bellied pigs, which are of exceptional quality. Down in the wine cellar, artisan cheeses are aging to perfection, as are the wines from the Pages' private label, Sweetbread Cellars. It seems wherever you look, something delicious is either being raised, aged, or ready to be trucked to the restaurant and butcher shop.

Over at La Boucherie, the menu changes weekly, depending on what's ready at the farm. That means you can expect to find ingredients that are always fresh, mainly organic, and packed with flavor. "Like our motto says: We farm it, raise it, harvest it, clean it, process it, cook it, and serve it!" says Kristin Page with a smile.

Given that farm-fresh pork is central to the restaurant's menu, La Boucherie

Executive Chef Dustin Calery shares two succulent pork chop preparations here. The first, Seared Pork Chop with Bacon Brussels Sprouts, Celeriac Puree & Apple Cider Butter, highlights the flavors of winter in the Northwest. Seattleites are fortunate to enjoy root vegetables, cabbages, and greens in the coldest months, while new crop apples and pears are also readily available. The second recipe, Summer Pork Chops with Grilled Sweet Corn Polenta & "Salsa Cotto," reflects a Northwest summer harvest in full swing, when the farmers' markets overflow with succulent Mediterranean vegetables.

Seared Pork Chop with Bacon Brussels Sprouts, Celeriac Puree & Apple Cider Butter

SERVES 4

Celeriac Puree:

1 tablespoon butter

2 medium onions, peeled and cut into ½-inch dice

1½ cups white stock (veal, chicken, or ham)

½ cup heavy cream

3 medium celeriac bulbs, cut into ¼-inch dice

Kosher salt and freshly ground black pepper to taste

Brussels Sprouts:

1 pound brussels sprouts, cored and julienned
   (see directions below)

1 tablespoon butter

1 medium onion, peeled and thinly julienned

4 strips of uncured, cooked bacon,
   cut into ½-inch pieces

Kosher salt and fresh ground black pepper to taste

½ cup white stock (veal, chicken, or ham)

Apple Cider Butter:

1½ cups unfiltered apple cider

4 tablespoons cold butter, cut into ¼-inch cubes

Kosher salt and fresh ground black pepper to taste

Pork Chops:

4 bone-in farmers' market free-range pork chops

Kosher salt and fresh ground black pepper to taste

2 tablespoons canola oil

Fresh apples, julienned, for garnish

Preheat the oven to 400°F.

To make the celeriac puree: In a medium saucepan over medium-high heat, combine the butter and onion and sauté until tender and translucent, taking care not to brown the onions. Add the stock and heavy cream and bring to a boil. Add the celeriac, and when the pan returns to a boil, reduce the heat to medium-low and cover. Allow to simmer for 20 minutes, stirring occasionally. When the celeriac is completely tender, remove from heat. Transfer the contents to a blender. With the top of the blender vented to avoid splatter, blend on low, then high, until completely smooth (if mixture is too thick, add a bit more stock). Season with salt and pepper and pulse again to thoroughly mix. Transfer back to saucepan and keep warm.

To make the brussels sprouts: With a paring knife, carefully remove the core of each sprout as you would the core of a tomato. Next, julienne the sprouts into about ⅛-inch slices. In a large skillet over medium-high heat, melt the butter until it sizzles, then add the onion, cooking until tender. Add the brussels sprouts, bacon, and some kosher salt and pepper and sauté, stirring constantly to avoid burning. When the edges of the sprouts start to just brown, add the stock, turn the burner down to low, stir the pan, and cover. Do not overcook! Overcooked brussels sprouts take on a sulfur flavor. Remove from heat.

To make the apple cider butter: Pour the cider into another saucepan and reduce by about two-thirds. Remove from heat and whisk in the cold butter, one or two cubes at a time, until fully incorporated. Adjust for seasoning (you can be liberal with the black pepper, as it complements the apples quite well). Keep in a warm, but not hot, place.

To make the pork chops: Season the chops with kosher salt and black pepper and allow to sit at room temperature for 1 hour. In a large oven-safe skillet on medium-high, heat the canola oil until it just reaches its smoke point (make sure you have the hood fan of your stove on high). Carefully place the chops in the pan, spacing them out evenly. Cook for about 3 minutes on one side and then carefully turn the chops over. Transfer the skillet to the preheated oven. In about 5 minutes, remove the pan from the oven and check the temperature of the chops. They are finished cooking when the internal temperature reaches 135°F (125°F for medium rare.) Move the pan to a warm place (the residual temperature of the pan will finish cooking the chops).

To serve: Ladle about ½ cup puree on the bottom of each of four large, warm bistro-style bowls (shallow and wide). Next, use tongs to equally distribute the finished brussels sprouts into attractive piles in the middle of the bowl. Rest the finished pork chops on the sprouts. Finally, spoon the desired amount of cider butter on and around the chops. Garnish with julienned fresh apples and serve.

Summer Pork Chops with
Grilled Sweet Corn Polenta & "Salsa Cotto"

Virtually everything in this recipe can be prepared on the grill on the day you choose to serve this dish. Only the polenta needs to be prepared in a kitchen using a saucepan, and this can easily be done the day before, in short order.

SERVES 6

Polenta:

6 strips of uncured bacon (found in the same place as the chops)

1 medium onion, peeled and cut into small dice

3 cups white stock (chicken, veal, or ham)

3 cobs fresh sweet corn

1 cup medium-grain polenta

4 tablespoons extra-virgin olive oil

¼ cup coarsely chopped fresh Italian parsley

Kosher salt and fresh ground black pepper to taste

Salsa Cotto:

6 large, ripe tomatoes (mixed heirlooms work well)

1 large sweet onion, peeled and cut across into 1-inch slices

4 mixed color bell peppers (preferably not green, as they tend to overpower)

Extra-virgin olive oil as needed

2 tablespoons chopped fresh oregano

¼ cup chopped fresh Italian parsley

1 garlic clove, peeled and crushed

1 tablespoon red wine vinegar

½ cup extra-virgin olive oil (a fruity olive oil suits this recipe well)

Kosher salt and fresh ground black pepper to taste

Pork Chops:

6 premium farmers' market free-range pork chops

Kosher salt and fresh ground black pepper to taste

2 tablespoons canola oil

Oregano sprigs for garnish

To make the polenta: In a heavy-bottom saucepan, sauté the bacon and onions on medium-high heat until the bacon starts to brown and the onions become translucent. Add the stock.

While the liquid comes to a boil, strip the kernels of corn from their cobs using a chef's knife or corn stripper. Take care not to cut into the tough cob.

When the stock boils, slowly whisk in the polenta and adjust heat to a very low simmer. Cook for 30 minutes, stirring constantly with a wooden spoon (the more it's stirred, the creamier it gets). Add the corn, and cook for 5 minutes more. Add the olive oil, parsley, salt, and pepper.

Turn out the polenta into a glass loaf pan, smooth the top, cover, and refrigerate until set, a few hours or overnight. Turn the chilled polenta out onto a cutting board. Cut into ½-inch slices and brush each slice with olive oil on both sides. Set aside.

To make the salsa cotto: Prepare and heat an outdoor grill. In a large bowl, toss the tomatoes, onion, and peppers with enough olive oil to coat (if you use too much, the oil will cause the grill to flare up, making the sauce taste like creosote). Place the tomatoes directly onto the grill and cook, gently turning until the skin is well browned and the flesh is soft. Carefully remove from the grill and place on a sheet pan to cool.

Next, place the onion slices on the grill and cook until well caramelized and tender, flipping them only once. Remove from the grill and add to the pan with the tomatoes.

Place the peppers on the grill and cook until most of the skin turns black and peppers are tender. Remove from grill and wrap in plastic wrap or place in a zipper storage bag (makes peeling much easier).

Remove the core and most of the skin from the cooled tomatoes, chop roughly, and add to the bowl the vegetables were initially tossed in. Next, rough chop the onions and add to the bowl. Retrieve the peppers from the bag or wrap and remove the peels, stems, core, and seeds. Rough chop and add to the bowl. Add the oregano, parsley, garlic, vinegar, olive oil, salt, and pepper. Mix thoroughly with a wooden spoon and set aside.

To make the pork chops: Season the chops with kosher salt and black pepper and allow to sit at room temperature for 1 hour. Brush canola oil onto a clean grill. Place the pork chops on the grill over medium-high temperature. Flip after 2 minutes, taking care to avoid flare-ups. Move the chops to a cooler part of the grill, or turn the gas off on the section of the grill where the pork chops are. Cover the grill and allow the pork chops to cook for about 5 minutes. With a meat thermometer, check the temperature. Remove chops from the grill when they reach an internal temperature of 130°F. Set aside to rest in a warm place.

Brush off the grill and turn the heat back up to medium high. While the chops are resting, place the polenta slices on the grill diagonally and cook for 5 minutes. Turn slices over and cook 5 minutes more or until heated through.

To serve: Place a slice of polenta slightly off center on each of six plates. Rest a pork chop atop the polenta. Spoon the sauce over the pork chop and a little more around the plate. Garnish with an oregano sprig and serve.

VASHON ISLAND

Vashon Island is a small isolated island, but the largest in Puget Sound and 60 percent larger than the city of Manhattan (but with many fewer residents—roughly ten thousand). There aren't any bridges that connect the island with the mainland, so trips to and from the isle are accomplished by taking one of two ferries. A number of farms operate on the island, providing locals with fresh organic produce, meats, milk, and eggs. The farms also make a point to sell their products to farmers' markets throughout Seattle. Vashon is also host to an annual Strawberry Festival. Since 1909 this popular festival attracts visitors from around the state and allows local growers the opportunity to showcase their fine berries. Vendors at the festival offer everything strawberry, from strawberry lemonade and strawberry sundaes, to strawberry funnel cakes, strawberry-topped pancakes, and chocolate-dipped strawberries.

PALISADE

2601 WEST MARINA PLACE, SEATTLE
(206) 285-1000
WWW.PALISADERESTAURANT.COM
OWNER: RESTAURANTS UNLIMITED INC.

When the sun is shining in Seattle, you will want to make a reservation at Palisade, whether for lunch, dinner, or their popular brunch. You'll be impressed with the classy ambience, the koi pond beneath your feet, and the spectacular views of the Elliott Bay Marina, downtown Seattle, and the Olympic Mountains as you peruse the restaurant's award-winning menu. Feel free to dine in the comfortable bar or relax on a sought-after window seat overlooking the shimmering sea. Whichever table you choose, you'll be equally impressed with the food, which is absolutely sensational and truly embodies Pacific Northwest cuisine, with a tropical flare.

Although Palisade is known for its abundant seafood (the tuna is flown in from Hawaii daily), its meats and poultry are just as superior. The prime rib and local rack of lamb are perfectly slow spit roasted over applewood, while the popular filet mignon and New York steaks are carefully chargrilled and accompanied by house-made sauces. The recipe featured here—Macadamia Nut Chicken—is a departure from the restaurant's often-requested items but a classic favorite from the original 1992 Palisade menu. Tender breasts of chicken are roasted to perfection, topped with macadamia nuts, and served with a Polynesian-inspired banana papaya chutney. Thanks to Palisade's equatorial-inspired cuisine, you can also enjoy delicious Pupu Towers and classic warm-weather libations like mai tais, coladas, mojitos, and ritas, which are handcrafted using 100 percent blue agave silver tequila. For wine lovers, the wine list will not disappoint, and there's always a wine steward a step away should you need a recommendation.

Macadamia Nut Chicken

SERVES 4

Beurre Blanc Sauce:

1 tablespoon white wine vinegar

½ cup white wine

½ tablespoon minced shallots

¼ cup heavy cream

1½ sticks unsalted butter, cut into small cubes

¼ teaspoon kosher salt

1 pinch white pepper

Banana Papaya Chutney:

½ cup peeled and finely diced red onion

½ cup finely diced red bell pepper

½ cup finely diced yellow pepper

1 tablespoon peeled and minced fresh ginger

½ cup brown sugar

4 whole cloves

Salt and pepper to taste

1 cup white wine vinegar

1 tablespoon light corn syrup

¼ cup raisins

3 cups coarsely chopped banana

2 cups coarsely chopped, peeled,
   and seeded papaya

Marinade:

1 ounce fresh minced ginger

¼ teaspoon minced garlic

Juice from half lemon

Pinch dried thyme

2 tablespoons olive oil

Salt and pepper to taste

Chicken:

4 chicken breasts, 6 or 7 ounces each,
   split lengthwise and pounded lightly

Salt and pepper, to taste

1 pound cooked jasmine rice

1 pound snap peas, cooked

¼ cup chopped macadamia nuts

4 tablespoons green onions, bias sliced ⅛-inch strips

To make the beurre blanc sauce: Combine the vinegar, white wine, and shallots in a saucepan. Bring to simmer over medium heat. Reduce the liquid to a light syrup (approximately 90 percent). Add the cream and continue to reduce, being careful not to scorch the sauce. Reduce the heat to low and slowly add and whip in the butter cubes. Season with salt and white pepper, then strain the sauce through a fine mesh strainer. Keep the sauce warm.

To make the banana papaya chutney: Combine the onion, peppers, ginger, brown sugar, cloves, salt, pepper, vinegar, and corn syrup in a heavy saucepan. Bring to a slow simmer over medium-high heat. Reduce the heat to low and let cook until a medium syrup consistency is achieved and the sauce is amber to light caramel in color.

Add the raisins, bananas, and papayas. Let slowly simmer until fruit is just tender. Do not overwork the chutney during the reduction process. The goal is to keep the bananas and papaya pieces intact.

To make the marinade: Place all the marinade ingredients in a mixing bowl and mix well to combine.

To make the chicken: Dip the chicken breasts into the marinade and then place into a preheated nonstick frying pan over medium-high heat. Season with salt and pepper. Turn the chicken over, season with more salt and pepper and let sear until the chicken is just done.

To serve: Mound some rice in the center of each serving plate and place the cooked snap peas above it. Prop the chicken breast halves, slightly overlapping, on the front side of the rice. Drizzle about 1 tablespoon beurre blanc sauce over the chicken and place a dollop of chutney on the top where the chicken pieces overlap. Sprinkle the top of the chutney with chopped macadamia nuts, top the macadamia nuts with sliced green onions, and serve.

Sweet Finishes

Seattle desserts rely heavily on in-season local fruits, berries, honey, nuts, and dairy products. The decadent dishes in this chapter emphasize the importance of using such ingredients while illustrating the creativity of some of the most talented pastry chefs working in Seattle and the Eastside's restaurants, cafes, and bakeries today.

Basil's Kitchen, located in downtown Bellevue, uses classic Northwest ingredients to make fabulous simple treats like Northwest Black Cherry Crème Brûlée and Blackberry-Rhubarb Cobbler. Fuji Bakery prides itself on using organic milk and eggs in its Cake Citron and Reauleau Caramel Chocolat. Harvest Vine also incorporates fresh local ingredients in a south-of-the-border–style rice pudding and flan made with—what else?—Seattle espresso. The Herbfarm, one of America's original farm-to-table restaurants, and National Geographic's pick for the "#1 Destination Restaurant in the World," rolls out a dessert from its fairy-tale farmhouse that truly symbolizes the Pacific Northwest—Douglas Fir Sorbet, made with real pine needles!

Along the shores of Lake Washington, a long-beloved but now closed restaurant, Madison Park Café was adamant about fresh local berries in its popular Clafoutis and Vanilla Bean Crème Brûlée. Along the same lines Matt's in the Market, located at the epicenter of Seattle's iconic Pike Place Market, infuses fresh maple syrup in a to-die-for crème brûlée. Its bread pudding is deliciously unique, too, with the addition of freshly roasted butternut squash.

Across the bridge on the Eastside, Chef Bradley Dickinson and Pearl Bar & Dining take advantage of the locally grown fruit as well as the Bellevue downtown farmers' market. Washington State's bounty of gorgeous, seasonal fruits help make desserts at Pearl a treat for all the senses. Enjoy freshly made fritters with local berries and bread pudding with sweet brown-sugar peaches. Finishing on the Eastside, Redmond's Regent Bakery & Café chooses to feature a traditional and not-so-traditional dessert with its fresh-baked oatmeal cookies and a surprisingly good green tea cheesecake.

BASIL'S KITCHEN

300 112TH AVENUE SOUTHEAST, BELLEVUE
(425) 455-1300
WWW.BELLEVUEHILTON.COM
OWNER: THE DOW HOTEL COMPANY

For business travelers, or those just needing to get away, many descend upon Hilton's Bellevue Hotel. Inside the casual-yet-sophisticated resort, which is often a mainstay for Microsoft recruits, Basil's Kitchen stays busy serving up delicious food to its guests at all hours of the day.

A blend of Mediterranean and Northwest cuisine, Basil's Kitchen and its welcoming interior and soothing ambience within the hotel atrium transport you to a sunny European cafe as you enjoy the lingering aromas of a wonderful meal. Using fresh, highest-quality ingredients enhanced by fresh herbs and simple preparations, Chef Favio Gomez—a member of the American Culinary Federation and the prestigious "Les Toques Blanches" International Club—creates attractive breakfast, lunch, and dinner menus that draw you in. Chef Gomez also prepares original culinary delights, including extraordinary desserts that infuse the flakiest of crusts and the creamiest of fillings with fresh fruits perfectly ripened by Mother Nature.

Here Chef Gomez shares his two favorite desserts of "foods you love." His Northwest Black Cherry Crème Brûlée and Blackberry-Rhubarb Cobbler are fabulous-but-simple treats that exemplify the Great Northwest.

NORTHWEST BLACK CHERRY CRÈME BRÛLÉE

SERVES 6

1 quart heavy cream
1 cup granulated sugar, divided
1 vanilla bean
12 egg yolks
8 ounces dried black cherries

Pour the heavy cream and half the sugar into a double boiler. Use a candy thermometer to make sure the temperature is 200°F. Using a knife, carefully split the vanilla bean in half and scrape the inside of the beans into the cream. Make sure the cream does not boil.

In a separate bowl, add the egg yolks and remaining sugar. Whisk well to emulsify. With the cream at temperature, whisk the egg mixture into the cream. Add the cherries, remove from heat, and allow mixture to cool completely. When cool, pour the mixture into six 6-ounce ceramic dishes or ramekins. Place the ramekins in a deep pan and transfer to a preheated 350°F oven. Fill the pan with 2 inches of water and cover ramekins and pan with a sheet of aluminum foil. Bake for 30 minutes. The texture should be stiff but should never boil during cooking.

BELLEVUE

Across Lake Washington from Seattle sits Bellevue, a burgeoning city that ranks as the second-largest city in Washington and one of the wealthiest cities in the state. According to recent polls, Bellevue also ranks among the top five places to live in America.

Bellevue (French for "beautiful view") has become a small version of Seattle, with excellent shopping and art museums and a long list of extraordinary restaurants, many of which serve traditional Pacific Northwest cuisine. There's also Bellevue Farmers' Market, which supports small family farms by providing a great place to sell farm-fresh foods directly to consumers. Delicious items include a variety of salad and lettuce mixes, greens and vegetables, fresh herbs, wild mushrooms, berries, fruit, artisan breads, cheeses, honey, jams, seafood, organic meats, pies, vinegars, and more.

BLACKBERRY-RHUBARB COBBLER

SERVES 4

Streusel Topping:

1 pound soft butter

1½ cups brown sugar

1⅓ cups quick oats

1 cup all-purpose flour

Cobbler:

2 pints fresh blackberries

1 cup diced rhubarb

3 cups apple juice

½ cup sugar

1 pinch nutmeg

1 whole clove

2 teaspoons cornstarch (mixed with a little water to create a slurry)

3 plain muffins, crumbled

To make the streusel topping: Place all the streusel topping ingredients in a mixing bowl and mix well to combine. Set aside.

To make the cobbler: In a saucepan over medium heat, combine the blackberries, rhubarb, apple juice, sugar, nutmeg, and clove. Bring to a boil, then lower the heat and reduce by a third. Add the cornstarch slurry and mix well. Remove from heat, add the crumbled muffins, and mix well.

Preheat the oven to 350°F. Divide the cobbler mixture among 4 ramekins. Top each with streusel topping, place in the oven, and bake for 10 minutes, or until the top is golden brown.

Fuji Bakery

526 S. King Street, Seattle
(206) 623-4050
www.fujibakeryinc.com
Owner: Akihiro Nakamura

It doesn't matter if you're dropping into the downtown Seattle bakery or the one across the floating bridge in Bellevue, as you'll find high-quality breads and exceptional cakes at both Fuji Bakery locations.

"Each of our bakery's creations starts with an idea that is given time to rise and take shape long before the bread itself does," says Head Chef Taka Hirai, who believes what he does is not a job—it's a calling. Accompanied by his pâtissier extraordinaire, Yushi Osawa, Fuji Bakery brings to the table not only years of training in France, Japan, and the United States, but a dedication to its craft evident in the thought and time put into the work. If you don't believe it, sink your teeth into one of their decadent chocolate croissants or moist focaccias, and you'll see what they're talking about. Guided by years of experience and a love for what they do, Fuji's craftspeople are intent upon producing flavorful breads and fluffy cakes that delight the imagination as well as the senses.

"Because we want to provide the freshest and healthiest food possible," adds Osawa, "we pride ourselves on premium ingredients that go into our products." From organic milk and eggs to imported Japanese flour, and from organic fruits when in season to European butter, Fuji Bakery is committed to using the best available ingredients to match the heart that goes into its baked goods. The chef's natural levain bread is made with additive-free leavening cultivated over months for deeper flavor, and the custards and other fillings are all made in-house. From its Bergamot-Infused Lemon Cake to its Almond Cream Pear Danish, Fuji Bakery creations are a delicious new take on what it means to be bread.

Cake Citron

MAKES 1 LARGE LOAF OR 3 PETITE LOAVES

Lemon Syrup:

6 tablespoon fresh lemon juice

Slightly less than ½ cup water

7½ tablespoons sugar

A few drops of bergamot essence

Cake:

½ cup sugar

1/3 cup fresh lemon zest

4 eggs

7 tablespoons plus some additional softened
    unsalted European butter

¼ cup heavy whipping cream

4 tablespoons citrus-infused rum

Slightly less than 1 cup cake flour

½ cup high-gluten flour

1 teaspoon baking powder

2/3 cup candied lemon peel

A few drops of bergamot essence (can be
    found at Whole Foods)

Preheat the oven to 375°F.

To make the lemon syrup: Place all the lemon syrup ingredients in a mixing bowl and whisk well to combine.

To make the cake: In a mixing bowl, whisk together sugar and lemon zest; set aside. In a separate bowl, beat the eggs and then use a whisk to combine the eggs with the sugar mixture. Now begin adding the egg and sugar mixture to another bowl containing the softened butter, pouring the mixture in a little at a time and whisking quickly after each addition to incorporate.

In yet another bowl, combine the cream and rum and then pour this into the main mixture in about three batches while whisking to combine.

In another bowl, sift together the cake flour, high-gluten flour, and baking powder and add this to the main mixture, using a spatula to stir with as few strokes as possible. Add the candied lemon peel and bergamot essence.

Pour the mixture into a large (9¼ x 5¼ x 2½-inch) loaf pan or three petite loaf pans. Pipe a line of softened butter down the center using a pastry bag or break off small squares of butter with your hands and place down the center. Bake for about 45 minutes. After baking, glaze with the lemon syrup. Let the cake sit overnight to allow the syrup to fully permeate the cake before serving.

Reauleau Caramel Chocolat

MAKES 1 CAKE (ABOUT 12 SERVINGS)

Biscuit Chocolat:

5 egg yolks

2 tablespoons plus 2 teaspoons sugar

5 egg whites

½ cup sugar, divided

2 tablespoons plus 2 teaspoons cornstarch

6 tablespoons cocoa powder

1½ ounces dark chocolate

3 tablespoons unsalted butter

Chantilly Caramel:

1 cup sugar

1¾ cup heavy whipping cream

Preheat the oven to 400°F.

To make the biscuit: In a small saucepan over low heat, combine the egg yolks and 2 tablespoons plus 2 teaspoons sugar and heat until lukewarm (around body temperature). Remove from the heat, then mix with an electric mixer until the color lightens.

In a separate bowl and with an electric mixer on high speed, whip ¼ cup sugar with half the egg whites for about 2 minutes, until the resultant meringue is stiff enough so that peaks form when you dip a spoon in and out. Repeat with the remaining ¼ cup sugar and egg whites, then combine with the first batch. In a separate small bowl, combine the cornstarch and cocoa powder.

Slowly fold the egg yolk mixture and cocoa powder mixture into the meringue.

In another bowl heat the chocolate and butter in the microwave until melted and lukewarm. Fold the chocolate mixture into the meringue and then pour out evenly into a medium (15 x 10-inch) baking sheet lined with parchment paper. Bake for 15–17 minutes.

To make the caramel: Heat the sugar and cream separately, both over low heat. Once the sugar becomes a uniform dark golden brown, turn off the heat and slowly mix in the boiling cream. After the mixture cools, refrigerate overnight. The next day, whip the mixture until it is light and fluffy.

To serve: Remove the biscuit from the parchment paper and place onto a larger fresh sheet. Pour the caramel over the biscuit, spreading out evenly with a spatula. Use the parchment paper to roll up the biscuit and caramel into a roll cake shape, and then slice and serve.

Harvest Vine

2701 East Madison Street, Seattle
(206) 320-9771
WWW.HARVESTVINE.COM
Owners: Joseba Jimenez de Jimenez and Carolin Messier de Jimenez

For Seattleites and those visiting Seattle, come to Harvest Vine for incredible Spanish-influenced foods, fine wines, and some of the best tapas in town.

Dining at the bar is perfect for small groups, because everyone can admire the chefs preparing the meals in the open exhibition kitchen. The restaurant is a bit deceiving upon arrival, especially for large parties who might think there's not enough room, but the cozy space opens up downstairs, beautifully accented with wine bottles and cellar decor.

The menu is short and rather simple, but don't let that fool you. With dishes such as Lamb Loin Foie Gras, Baby Octopus, and Steamed Clams, you can be assured you'll be feasting on wonderfully fresh and savory meats and seafood.

Of course, one cannot mention Harvest Vine without boasting about their incredibly sinful desserts. From their Tarta de Pinones, a pine nut tart with quince paste, and Tarta de Aceite y Vino, an olive oil cake with poached pears and Chantilly cream, to their heavenly Brazo Gitano, chocolate cake, chocolate mousse, and blood oranges in a red wine reduction, the sweet treats here will have you coming back for more.

Featured here for the home cook are the often-requested Flan de Cafe—considered one of the best desserts on the menu—creamy espresso custard with ganache, and the popular Arroz con Leche, warm cinnamon rice pudding. Enjoy!

Arroz con Leche

RICE PUDDING

SERVES 4

1 tablespoon butter
1 cup bomba rice (Spanish paella rice)
6 cups milk, divided
2 cinnamon sticks, broken
Zest of 2 lemons
¾ cup cream
½ cup sugar
1 tablespoon cinnamon

In a stainless steel saucepan over medium heat, melt the butter and briefly sauté the rice until it is completely covered with the butter. Cover with 2 cups milk and add the cinnamon sticks and lemon zest. Bring to a boil, then simmer on medium heat. Slowly add the rest of the milk, occasionally stirring to keep from burning. After all the milk has been cooked into the rice, stir in the cream and sugar and cook for a few more minutes. Remove the cinnamon sticks, sprinkle the pudding with cinnamon, and serve warm.

This recipe can also be refrigerated and served cold.

Flan de Cafe

SERVES 4

Flan:

1 quart heavy cream
½ zest of an orange
3 large eggs
9 egg yolks
1¼ cup sugar
1½ cups milk
½ cup espresso
⅓ cup brandy

Caramel:

1 cup sugar
¼ cup water

To make the flan: In a stainless steel pot, slowly heat the cream with the orange zest. While the cream is heating, mix the eggs with the yolks in a large bowl. Quickly stir the sugar in with the eggs and mix well. Slowly stir in the heated cream, then add the milk, espresso, and brandy. Cool down the mixture and strain.

To make the caramel: In a saucepan over medium-high heat, combine the sugar and water and cook until the sugar is liquefied and caramel in color. While hot, pour the caramel into twelve 4-ounce ramekins until the bottom of each is just covered. Let the caramel cool, then pour the flan mixture into each ramekin.

Preheat the oven to 300°F. Place the ramekins into a large baking dish. (Use a pan that's large enough to allow for some space between the ramekins.) Slowly pour cold water around the outside of the ramekins to form a water bath. Place in the oven and cook for 1½ hours. Remove from the oven and cool.

To serve: Run a paring knife around the outside of each flan and carefully invert the flan onto a serving plate.

The Herbfarm

14590 Northeast 145th Street, Woodinville
(425) 485-5300
www.theherbfarm.com
Owners: Ron Zimmerman and Carrie Van
Dyck

The Herbfarm in Woodinville is an award-winning
restaurant, a garden, a home, and a culinary oasis all
wrapped into one.

Despite humble beginnings in a garage in 1986, the
restaurant—now housed in a picturesque farmhouse—is
the only Five Diamond restaurant north of San Francisco
and west of Chicago. A day at the Herbfarm begins early
down on its farm when the still-warm eggs are collected,
the ducks and chickens fed, the pigs scratched, and the
first early morning pickers go through the fields gathering
what the chefs have requested overnight. The morning's
treasure is whisked the mile-and-a-half trek to the
restaurant, where the awaiting cooks begin the daily food
prep leading up to the night's nine-course dinner paired
with six Northwest wines.

Founded by Carrie Van Dyck and Ron Zimmerman,
the James Beard Award–winning restaurant continues
to rank as one of the best destination restaurants in the
United States—even surpassing California's famous
French Laundry and Chez Panisse. That's because
everything is fresh and made from scratch. The restaurant
churns its own butter, cures meat, crafts cheese, makes
sea salt from Pacific waters, and ferments its breads
with native yeast. Wild foraged foods, mushrooms, and
truffles complement the local seafood, farm vegetables,
and meat and game farmed to its exacting specifications.
It's no surprise diners come from near and far to cherish
a meal handcrafted by the Herbfarm. Even if that means
savoring a spoonful of homemade sorbet made with
the tips of local fir trees. It's true, and we have the prized
recipe here to prove it!

Douglas Fir Sorbet

SERVES UP TO 20 AS AN INTERMEZZO OR DESSERT

1 cup sugar

3 cups water

4 cups rinsed fresh Douglas fir tips (the last
    4 to 6 inches)

¼ cup lemon juice

1 cup champagne or sparkling wine

Bring the sugar and water to a boil in a medium saucepan. Add the evergreen tips, remove from heat, and let the mixture steep for 1 hour.

Strain the syrup through a fine sieve. Add the lemon juice and champagne or sparkling wine. Freeze the mixture in an ice-cream maker and serve when ready.

For a coarser-textured granite, put the mix in a metal bowl in the freezer and stir it every half hour to break up the ice crystals.

FIR TREES

Douglas firs are evergreen coniferous trees found throughout the Pacific Northwest. They grow from 60 to 350 feet tall and are commonly marketed as Christmas trees throughout the United States. Other holiday species include noble firs and grand firs.

The idea for this unique sorbet recipe came to the Herbfarm many years ago, when friend Nancy Turner, an ethnobotanist at the University of British Columbia, mentioned that the Coast Salish Indians used to brew a tea from the tips of Douglas Firs. It turns out the fir tips are high in vitamin C, just the thing for a cold. This delightful treat can be made with any kind of fir, including Douglas fir, grand fir, alpine fir, noble fir, and balsam fir. Although refreshing and unique any time of year, the Herbfarm guests find it particularly welcome during the holidays.

MADISON PARK CAFE

1807 42ND AVENUE EAST, SEATTLE
OWNER: KAREN BINDER

Owner Karen Binder opened Madison Park Cafe in 1979 as a relaxing place to sip fresh-brewed coffee and tea. As the Madison Park community grew, so did her cafe. Before she knew it, Karen's cafe became the quintessential neighborhood restaurant, serving some of Seattle's finest French bistro dinners and cocktails.

Taking a break from the kitchen, Karen shifted her role to concentrate on the restaurant's wine list. She incorporated many French wines to her menu. Some quipped her cafe was better known for the wine selection than the food.

Because of the homey feeling the restaurant provided, patrons could sit inside by the cozy fireplace, which dates back to 1924. Weather permitting, one could also dine outdoors on the cobblestone courtyard, which made for a wonderful "backyard" setting.

Besides the decadent desserts, the mussels at Madison Park Cafe were considered the best in town, according to Citysearch, and the French onion soup and cassoulet were signature dishes and benchmarks for what Madison Park dining is truly about.

Chef Rich Coffey, who joined the kitchen in 2007 as a pastry chef, shares his famous Clafoutis and Vanilla Bean Crème Brûlée recipes here.

Addressing her faithful supporters and culinary friends, Madison Park Cafe owner Karen Binder recently announced she has sold her charming restaurant after thirty-two years of operation. As many locals know, especially those residing in Madison Park, Karen's cafe was the neighborhood place to visit for exceptional breakfasts, including real sourdough pancakes, weekend brunches, and all-around good food—particularly its desserts—complemented by warm, friendly hospitality.

But the kitchen burners are not turned off entirely. Karen sold her cafe to Seattle chef Celinda Norton, better known as the celebrated chef behind 94 Stewart at Pike Place Market. Now operating in the same quaint building as Madison Park Cafe, Celinda is busy serving the Madison Park community with deliciously creative New World Italian dishes at the newly named Cafe Parco bistro.

CLAFOUTIS

SERVES 4–6

2 eggs
2 egg yolks
½ cup granulated sugar
¼ cup all-purpose flour
1½ cups crème fraîche (can substitute sour cream)
1 vanilla bean
1 pint fresh fruit (cherries, blueberries, raspberries,
    apples, peaches; avoid fruits that have excessive
    juice, such as strawberries)

Preheat the oven to 375°F.

Combine the eggs, egg yolks, sugar, and flour in a mixing bowl and whisk thoroughly to break up any clumps of flour. Whisk in the crème fraîche. Slice open the vanilla bean and scrape out the small seeds from the inside (reserve the outer pod for another use, such as vanilla sugar). Whisk the vanilla seeds into the mixture.

Butter an 8- or 9-inch-square glass or ceramic baking dish and give it a light coating of flour. (You can also use individual baking dishes if you prefer.) Place the fruit in the baking dish and pour the flour mixture over the fruit. Bake the clafoutis until it rises and browns, about 30 to 40 minutes. Allow more baking time if the clafoutis seems to have too much liquid in the center. The clafoutis should settle once it begins to cool after baking.

Serve warm with a scoop of ice cream, or serve cold if you desire.

Vanilla Bean Crème Brûlée

SERVES 4

7 egg yolks
1 egg
1 quart heavy whipping cream
1½ cups granulated sugar, plus extra for caramelizing
1 fresh vanilla bean
Fresh berries, for garnish

Whisk the egg yolks and egg together in a large mixing bowl. Pour the cream into a saucepan and whisk in the sugar. Slice the vanilla bean open and scrape out the inside; add both the insides and the bean to the cream mixture. Over medium-high heat, bring the cream mixture up to scalding, whisking lightly to be sure the sugar is completely melted. When the sugar is melted, temper the cream mixture into the egg mixture, whisking frequently to avoid cooking the eggs. Strain the mixture through a fine strainer.

Preheat the oven to 350°F.

Gather together four ceramic baking dishes such as soufflé molds or ramekins. Place the baking dishes into a large baking pan such as a casserole pan. Use a pan that's large enough to allow for some space between the baking dishes (about 9 x 13 x 2 inches). Using a pitcher or ladle, fill each baking dish almost to the top with the custard mixture. Then pour cold water around the outside of the dishes to form a water bath. Cover tightly with foil and carefully slide the pan into the preheated oven.

The baking time will vary depending on the oven and baking dishes, so check after 30 minutes. Open the foil with extreme caution as to avoid a steam burn. Jiggle the custard a bit; it should not be liquid inside, but rather jiggly like gelatin. If the custard is still liquid, return to the oven and continue to cook. Avoid letting the custard boil, as this will ruin the dessert.

When the custards are ready, move them to the refrigerator and allow to cool completely, at least 2 hours but ideally overnight.

To serve: Cover the top of each custard with about 1/16 inch granulated sugar and caramelize the sugar with a kitchen torch (or under a broiler). Top with some fresh berries to finish.

Matt's in the Market

94 Pike Street, #32, Seattle
(206) 467-7909
www.mattsinthemarket.com
Owner: Dan Bugge

Seattle's Pike Place Market is world famous. But tucked into the Corner Market Building is a thriving culinary gem that's famous with local residents and visitors who are lucky enough to stumble upon it. We're talking about Matt's in the Market, a bustling eatery that's always packed to the brim with hungry patrons, particularly shoppers in need of a rest and a delicious meal. (Note: Reservations are a must, as the wait line is often long.)

Matt's decor is simple, nothing extravagant or over the top, except for the spectacular views of the market and the beehive of activity that abounds below (always request a window seat—it's worth it). But what is over the top is the food. After all, Matt's does not have to travel far to acquire the finest and freshest ingredients from the Northwest. As further proof, a large chalkboard features what's in season.

Although the menu changes often, the food is consistently good. The house-made potato chips are always popular, as are the catfish sandwich, pork belly, and the prized lamb burger—widely believed to be the best in Seattle. Matt's also serves dinner, and you can never go wrong if you swing by during happy hour. The wine list is impressive, as are the cocktail selections and local beers on tap. The desserts, likes the two featured here, are equally divine. Loyal guests of Matt's often order the bread pudding and crème brûlée.

If you go, be sure to valet, as parking around the market is virtually obsolete, unless you like to walk.

BUTTERNUT SQUASH BREAD PUDDING

SERVES 6–8

1 butternut squash, ends removed, split, and seeded
1 small loaf of brioche bread, cut into 1-inch cubes
1 quart heavy whipping cream
¾ cup brown sugar
4 eggs
¼ teaspoon salt

Preheat the oven to 375°F.

Place the split and seeded butternut squash open side down on a parchment-lined baking sheet. Bake the squash for 30 to 45 minutes, or until a knife inserts easily into the squash. Cool and peel the squash, then puree in a food processor. Set aside and lower the oven temperature to 350°F.

Place the cubed bread into a large glass or ceramic baking dish.

Heat the cream and sugar in a large saucepan on the stove over medium heat. In a bowl, whisk together the eggs and salt. Add a small amount of the hot cream to the eggs, stirring vigorously. Once the egg is well incorporated, add the egg mixture back into the cream and stir to combine. Pour the custard over the cubed bread, then add half of the pureed butternut squash. Massage all the custard and squash into the bread, and then let it sit in the refrigerator to absorb for 1 hour. Depending on the dryness of the bread, add the rest of the squash puree if needed.

Cover the baking dish with foil and bake at 350°F until the internal temperature reaches 180°F.

Serve warm for breakfast or with ice cream for dessert.

MAPLE CRÈME BRÛLÉE

SERVES 4–6

1½ cups heavy whipping cream
½ cup maple syrup
1 vanilla bean, split and scraped
¼ teaspoon salt
4 egg yolks
Granulated sugar, as needed

Preheat the oven to 300°F.

In a saucepan over medium-high heat, combine the cream, maple syrup, vanilla bean, and salt and bring to a simmer. Whisk the egg yolks in a separate bowl. While whisking, add the hot cream mixture and continue to whisk until all the ingredients are incorporated.

Place 4 to 6 individual baking dishes or ramekins (4–6 ounces each) into a large baking pan such as a casserole pan. Use a pan that's large enough to allow for some space between the baking dishes (about 9 x 13 x 2 inches). Using a pitcher or ladle, fill each baking dish almost to the top with the cream mixture. Then pour cold water around the outside of the dishes to form a water bath. Cover tightly with foil and carefully slide the pan into the preheated oven.

The baking time will vary depending on the oven, baking dishes, and so on, so check after 30 minutes. Open the foil with extreme caution as to avoid a steam burn. Jiggle the custard a bit; it should not be liquid inside, but rather jiggly like gelatin. If the custard is still liquid, return to the oven and continue to cook. Avoid letting the custard boil, as this will ruin the dessert.

When the custards are ready, move them to the refrigerator and allow to cool completely, at least 2 hours but ideally overnight.

To serve: Cover the top of each custard with about ¹⁄₁₆ inch granulated sugar and caramelize the sugar with a kitchen torch (or under a broiler).

Pearl Bar & Dining

Lincoln Square
700 Bellevue Way NE, Suite 50, Bellevue
(425) 455-0181
www.pearlbellevue.com
Owners: Bradley Dickinson and Mikel Rogers

Pearl Bar & Dining, located in the heart of Bellevue, is a must for those who enjoy extraordinary food within a warmly lit "sexy" environment. Adorned with modern art and glass sculpture conversation pieces, the black-clad restaurant immediately feels like a chic Los Angeles or New York eatery with a nightclub feel. But once you settle inside, the atmosphere is engaging and inviting, and the food is sensational, which is why people come here—especially those with a sweet tooth.

"Washington State is blessed with a bounty of gorgeous, seasonal fruits that help make desserts at Pearl a treat for all the senses," says Executive Chef and Co-Proprietor Bradley Dickinson. "Fragrant, tree-ripened peaches, for example, are handpicked at the peak of juicy perfection, ensuring a natural sweetness that comes through in every bite. Deepened with brown sugar in baked desserts (such as the recipe showcased here), peaches become downright decadent (if not habit forming) as an after-dinner treat. Stone fruits, such as local, in-season apricots and nectarines, can stand in as worthy substitutes if you don't have peaches on hand."

Locally grown berries find their way into Pearl's freshly made fritters (also featured here) during the summer months. "Raspberries, strawberries, blueberries, and blackberries all grace the restaurant's desserts, as well as the occasional reduction, to complement the restaurant's savory dishes," adds the chef. "The color pops on the plate, while the berries' sweet and tart flavors burst with every bite. Be sure to change up the berries in the fritter recipe, as late spring and early summer turn out new fresh and sweet varieties."

Brown Sugar Peaches with Vanilla Bread Pudding

SERVES 4–6

Bread Pudding:

8 cups brioche or egg bread, cut into ¾-inch cubes

5 eggs, beaten

1¼ cups sugar

1 cup whole milk

1 cup whipping cream

2 teaspoons vanilla extract

1 tablespoon Amaretto liqueur, optional

Brown-Sugar Peaches:

2 medium-size ripe Washington-grown peaches, sliced

¼ cup brown sugar

1½ tablespoons soft butter

1–2 tablespoons water if needed

4–6 scoops vanilla ice cream

To make the bread pudding: Allow the bread cubes to dry out slightly and then place in a lightly buttered 4 x 9 loaf pan.

Place the eggs and sugar in a mixing bowl and mix well to combine. Add the milk, whipping cream, vanilla, and Amaretto, if using, and mix well. Pour this mixture over the bread in the loaf pan and allow to sit at room temperature for 30 minutes.

Preheat the oven to 325°F.

Place the bread pudding in the oven for approximately 50 minutes, or until a toothpick comes out dry. Allow to cool slightly.

To make the topping: In a saucepan over low heat, add the peaches, brown sugar, and butter and stir gently to combine. Allow the sugar to melt until it is caramelized. Add the water if the sauce is too thick. Heat the sauce thoroughly.

To serve: Arrange the bread pudding on serving plates. Top with vanilla ice cream and brown sugar peaches.

PEARL FRITTERS

SERVES 4–6

½ cup water

¼ cup butter

2 teaspoons sugar

½ cup flour

2 eggs

Vegetable oil, as needed

1 teaspoon honey

1 scoop vanilla ice cream

2 tablespoons plain yogurt

¼ cup fresh Northwest berries (blackberries, blueberries, or strawberries)

1 teaspoon brown sugar

¼ teaspoon orange zest

Combine the water, butter, and sugar in a saucepan over medium heat. Allow the butter to melt completely, mix well, and remove from heat.

Add the flour and mix well. Remove the dough from the pan and transfer to a mixer or food processor on medium-high speed. Add the eggs one at a time until thoroughly incorporated.

Heat the vegetable oil in a heavy stockpot or cast-iron skillet until it reaches 350°F on a deep-fry thermometer (oil should be at least 2 inches deep). Carefully place half-dollar-size scoops of batter into the oil and cook until the fritters are golden brown on all sides. Remove from the oil and allow to drain on paper towels.

Place the cooked fritters on a serving platter and drizzle with honey. Garnish with ice cream, yogurt, and berries. Sprinkle with brown sugar and fresh orange zest.

Regent Bakery & Cafe

15159 Northeast 24th Street, Redmond
(425) 378-1498
Owners: Teresa and Betty Loh

The Redmond neighborhood is best known as the home for Microsoft and its sprawling campus, but for foodies craving something sweet and delicious, Regent Bakery & Cafe owns the spotlight. While the small storefront sandwiched between two neighboring businesses and a strip mall may seem deceiving, head inside and you'll be pleasantly surprised.

Inside, the cafe is clean, friendly, and home to some of the best and most sought-after cakes in town. Many customers, some famous, phone in their order—particularly for the fruitcakes, soft handcrafted pastries, and creamy Japanese cheesecakes, which are made fresh every day. Others love the real whipped cream frosting (no cheap imitations here) or the Black Forest cake. And the dessert prices are very reasonable. Next time you're in the area, especially during a birthday, make sure to pick up a specialty cake from Regent's award-winning bakery. They're lighter, fluffier, and tastier than what you'll find at any local market. If you happen to be in Seattle, you're still in luck, as the Lohs recently opened a second Regent Bakery & Cafe on Capitol Hill, offering a similar assortment of decadent cakes, Chinese buns, and pastries.

"The two Regent recipes featured here—Oatmeal Cookies and Green Tea Cheesecake—are specifically designed for our customers," says Teresa Loh. "They are fun to make and can be prepared easily at home."

Oatmeal Cookies

MAKES 40 COOKIES

¾ cup softened butter

½ cup brown sugar

2 eggs

1 tablespoon condensed milk

2 cups all-purpose flour

1¾ cups oatmeal

½ cup raisins

In a large mixing bowl, combine the butter and brown sugar and beat well until thoroughly combined. Add the eggs and condensed milk and beat until combined. Slowly mix in the flour until combined. Add the oatmeal and raisins and mix fully by hand.

Place the cookie dough in the refrigerator and chill for 1 hour. After an hour, preheat the oven to 375°F. Remove the dough from the refrigerator and form into small balls, about the size of a quarter. Lay the dough balls on a greased baking sheet and press slightly. Bake for 16 minutes, or until edges are firm. Transfer the cookies to a wire rack and allow to cool.

Green Tea Cheesecake

1 (8-INCH) CAKE SERVES 2 TO 4

Crust:

2 cups crumbled Oreo cookies

½ cup melted butter

Cheesecake:

3¾ cups softened cream cheese

1/3 cup sugar

2 egg yolks

1 tablespoon green tea powder (available at Asian markets)

½ cup milk

1½ tablespoons gelatin

½ cup hot water

1 cup whipping cream

To make the crust: Combine the crumbled Oreo cookies with the melted butter in a mixing bowl. Stir well and set aside.

To make the cheesecake: In a large mixing bowl, beat the cream cheese with the sugar until fluffy. Add the egg yolks and beat until smooth. In a separate bowl, mix the green tea powder with the milk, then stir into the cheese mixture. In a separate bowl, dissolve the gelatin in the hot water, then stir into the cheese mixture. In another bowl, whip the whipping cream until stiff peaks form. Gently fold the whipped cream into the cheese mixture.

Place the crust in an 8-inch pan, mold, or baking ring. Pour the cheese mixture over the crust. Chill in the refrigerator until set.

Metric U.S. Approximate Equivalents

LIQUID INGREDIENTS

Metric	U.S. Measures	Metric	U.S. Measures
1.23 ml	¼ tsp.	29.57 ml	2 tbsp.
2.36 ml	½ tsp.	44.36 ml	3 tbsp.
3.70 ml	¾ tsp.	59.15 ml	¼ cup
4.93 ml	1 tsp.	118.30 ml	½ cup
6.16 ml	1¼ tsp.	236.59 ml	1 cup
7.39 ml	1½ tsp.	473.18 ml	2 cups or 1 pt.
8.63 ml	1¾ tsp.	709.77 ml	3 cups
9.86 ml	2 tsp.	946.36 ml	4 cups or 1 qt.
14.79 ml	1 tbsp.	3.79 l	4 qts. or 1 gal.

DRY INGREDIENTS

Metric	U.S. Measures	Metric	U.S. Measures
2 (1.8) g	1/16 oz.	80 g	2⅘ oz.
3½ (3.5) g	⅛ oz.	85 (84.9) g	3 oz.
7 (7.1) g	¼ oz.	100 g	3½ oz.
15 (14.2) g	½ oz.	115 (113.2) g	4 oz.
21 (21.3) g	¾ oz.	125 g	4½ oz.
25 g	⅞ oz.	150 g	5¼ oz.
30 (28.3) g	1 oz.	250 g	8⅞ oz.
50 g	1¾ oz.	454 g	1 lb. (16 oz.)
60 (56.6) g	2 oz.	500 g	1 livre (17⅗ oz.)

INDEX

Photo Credits

All food photography by Jessica Nicosia-Nadler. Other photos by . . .

page i Shutterstock.com © Steve Estvanik

page iii Shutterstock.com © Al Rublinetsky

page iv Shutterstock.com © Irina Silvestrova

page x Shutterstock.com © Ng Wei Keong

page xi Shutterstock.com © Liem Bahneman

page xii Shutterstock.com (clockwise from top left) © RonGreer.Com; © Mark B. Bauschke; © Steve Estvanik; © Dallas Events Inc

page xiii Shutterstock.com © Natalia Bratslavsky

page xiv © Purple Café and Wine Bar

page xv © Salty's

page xvi © Matt's in the Market

page 2 © Andaluca

pages 6 & 7 © Cactus

page 10 © Daniel's Broiler

pages 13 & 16 © Chandler's Crabhouse

page 17 © Joey Restaurants

pages 20, 21 & 23 © Purple Café & Wine Bar

page 24 Shutterstock.com © Sanyam Sharma

page 26 © SkyCity Restaurant

page 32 James O. Fraioli

page 33 © Ray's Boathouse

page 35 Shutterstock.com © Poul Costinsky

page 41 © Barking Frog

page 42 © John Granen

page 44 © Poppy

pages 46 & 47 © Volterra

page 48 Shutterstock.com © Marco Mayer

pages 50, 51 & 54 © Salish Lodge & Spa

pages 56 & 59 © Tilth Restaurant

page 63 © Bastille

page 64 Shutterstock.com

page 66 Shutterstock.com © Jeffrey M. Frank

page 69 © Assagio Ristorante

pages 72 & 73 © Bizzarro Italian Cafe

page 76 Shutterstock.com © p.studio66

page 77 © La Spiga

page 80 © Il Fornaio

page 84 © Palomino

page 88 © Salty's

page 90 © Barrio Mexican Kitchen & Bar

pages 92 & 95 © Kathryn Barnard

page 96 © Chef Holly Smith

pages 100 & 102 © Elliott's Oyster House

page 104 © Flying Fish

Page 105 James O. Fraioli

page 108 © Lara Ferroni

pages 112 & 113 © Trellis Restaurant

page 116 © Waterfront Seafood Grill

page 120 © Charity Lynn Photography

page 123 © Cicchetti Kitchen & Bar

page 124 © Coho Café

page 130 © El Gaucho

pages 131 & 133 © Metropolitan Grill

page 136 © Geoffrey Smith

page 140 © Earth & Ocean

page 143 © Charity Lynn Photography

page 149 © Libby Lewis

page 152 Shutterstock.com © Wiktory

page 154 © Natalia Bratslavsky

pages 159, 161 & 163 © Fuji Bakery

page 164 © Harvest Vine

pages 169, 170, 171 © Ron Zimmerman

page 173 © Madison Park Cafe

page 174 Shutterstock.com © sixninepixels

pages 176 & 177 © Matt's in the Market

page 179 Shutterstock.com © Anna Hoychuk

pages 182, 183, 185 © Regent Bakery & Cafe

page 192 Brian Hodges Photography

About the Author

James O. Fraioli (pronounced fray-o-lee) is an award-winning cookbook author of seventeen titles, with additional cookbooks currently in production. Fraioli's cookbooks have been featured on The Food Network and *The Ellen DeGeneres Show,* and have been given as gifts to members of the White House staff. The author is known for teaming up with celebrity chefs and world-renowned restaurants to showcase the best the culinary world has to offer. Participating chefs over the years include James Beard Award–winners John Ash, Tom Douglas, Bradley Ogden, Jacques Pepin, and Holly Smith, as well as Emeril Lagasse and Roy Yamaguchi. Fraioli's cookbooks have also appeared on dozens of national radio shows, including Martha Stewart Living Radio and *Dining Around with Gene Burns.* The author's beautiful and well-crafted books, continually noted for their exceptional prose, high  production value, exquisite photography, and savory subject matter, have received further praise from such esteemed periodicals as *Forbes Traveler, Reader's Digest,* the *San Francisco Chronicle,* and the *New York Times.* Visit him on the web at www.culinarybookcreations.com.